Fully Prepped?

A Comprehensive Guide to What You Need to be Prepared

Todd Jones

OTHER BOOKS BY TRIUMPH PRESS

The Triumph Book by Melanie Davis

The Triumph Book: HEROES by Melanie Davis and 27 Veterans

The Triumph Program by Melanie Davis

The Triumph Program: **Military Edition**
by Melanie Davis and Matthew Brown USMC

A Soldiers Journey and the Battle Within by Cleo DeLoner

*Healing the Warrior Heart: A Glimpse into the Hearts of Combat Veterans
and their Supporting Loved Ones*
by Andrew R. Jones USMC Combat Veteran

*Finding Your Voice - Thriving as a Woman in the Military:
Tools for Success* by TF SASS with Melanie Davis

A Combat Nightmare in WWII by LTC Julian A Roadman

*My Brother in Arms: The Exceptional Life of Mark Andrew Forester,
United States Air Force Combat Controller* by Thad Forester

Triumph Press is a resource for those who have the
passion to tell their life-stories and change the world.
If you have a true and inspiring story to share, visit
www.TriumphPress.com to learn how we can help you
publish and join our library of inspirational books.

Message from the Publisher

You have purchased the *Fully Prepped?* workbook because you know the importance of being prepared and I have published it for the same reason. The information found in this book is vital. An emergency or disaster situation can happen at any time, to anyone; and the potential for it to affect those around us is just as great. In fact, we are actually only as ready and *safe* as our neighbors are prepared. Taking the time to meet with your neighbors to discuss, think through and gather the food, water and materials needed should a crisis or extended shut down of traditional services occur can mean the difference between a community that pulls together and one where violence and panic erupts. Unfortunately, we have already seen this chaos and death happen in the natural disasters which have struck in the recent past. For this reason, Triumph Press and Todd Jones are offering bulk discounts for the purchase of this workbook through our *Neighborhood Network Program*, so that it can become a tool for communication and preparation between neighbors and within communities.

Please visit www.EffectiveTactics.com to see the deeply discounted rates for buying bulk quantities in packages of 6, 12 or 24 books, with the price reducing as the numbers go up. These discounts are only available at this website.

Thank you for taking the time to be Fully Prepped!
Melanie Davis

Founder of Triumph Press and co-host with Todd Jones on the Effective Tactics radio show

This guide is for both beginners and seasoned Preppers. It will aid you in planning, shopping and tracking your supplies. It will help newbies get started and experts be more organized. Do you know how much bleach is needed to purify water? It's in here. Know what to pack into a first aid kit? Yep, got that too. When you're told to evacuate, what do you do first? You'll find that here also. This guide can help you overcome the fear of getting started. It can also give you the edge you need to survive when disaster strikes. *–Todd Jones*

PRAISE FOR FULLY PREPPED

Think you're ready? So did I, until I read this book. Then, I realized that although I am better prepared than most, I still had holes in my plan. Fully Prepped is chock full of good information anyone interested in formulating a survival and continuation plan shouldn't be without. Get this book, read this book, share this book. You'll be glad you did

John H. - ShieldTactical.com - TBRCI.com

I might be the very opposite of Todd; I don't talk about lists at the Tin Hat Ranch too often. Sure, I use them, but my intent is to get people writing their own lists. Yet it is Todd's methodical lists that hooked me. What am I missing? This book is a very well thought out, comprehensive look at prepping that must be years in the making. *Fully Prepped* is a must have for anyone who wishes to be prepared in today's uncertain times, whether you have just awakened to the fact you need to be ready, or are a well-seasoned prepper, there is something in it for you. I'd considered writing my own book on prepping, but I don't know if I could top Todd's; from now on I will refer folks to *Fully Prepped*.

Mike K. Owner - TinHatRanch.com

Todd Jones has grabbed my attention with his book *Fully Prepped*. This book is a valuable guide for the seasoned prepper and new ones alike. This is a very well written book that has everything in it! I'd like to think of myself as ready for anything life throws my way, but after reading *Fully Prepped*, I now know that there are plans I over looked and gaps in other areas. Not only does he keep my attention, but I can see he has values and principals in what he has written. *Fully Prepped* is definitely going in my collection.

April G. - https://facebook.com/StrengthandBeyond

Not every American will accept being called "a prepper," but EVERY American needs to be prepared for the eventualities of daily life and of disasters (man-made and natural). Todd has written a truly useful guide for average people to be able to maximize their preparedness in practical and simple ways. Read it and use the principles and advice he gives to be the family that not only survives the next disaster, but thrives through it.

John C. - ActiveSelfProtection.com

Finally a book created for everyone! Todd has put a detailed guide together for prepper newbies and veterans alike. All parties can benefit from *Fully Prepped* which is a wealth of information. Regardless of whether you're a prepper, someone wanting to be prepared for a natural disaster, camper, or hunter, this book is a must have.

Ron D. Owner - BlackTydeTactical.com

DEDICATION

I would like to thank my Lord for giving me the skill set to make this piece of work possible

I would like to dedicate this book to my family and friends.
Without their encouragement I never would have taken on this task.
Allie, Craig, Robert, Richard, and Dorothy,
Thanks for the push!

FOREWORD

Having been involved in safety and survival training for three decades, it is safe to say that I have seen, heard or read plenty of articles, manuals and how-to books on the subject. From my time in the United States Air Force, as an instructor and course developer for a major airline and the founder of a tactical training school there are two things that always determine the effectiveness of training materials: is it factual and is it useful?

In *Fully Prepped*, Todd Jones hits the nail on the head! The information is practical, comprehensive and most of all, easy to grasp while being entertaining enough to keep the reader engaged.

I'm sure this is one book that will make its way into the courses at our school and as a take-away for our students. You will be doing your family a huge service by applying this information to your emergency plans and keeping another copy in your Bug Out Bag!

Jim Peterson
Operations Manager and Founder
Advantage Tactical Company, LLC

Every Saturday Before Veterans Day Is

The National Love Your Veterans Range Day!

Go to *www.LoveYourVeterans.org* to learn about the
Annual National Love Your Veterans Range Day
And join the **Shooters Association**!

Sponsored by

TABLE OF CONTENTS

EMERGENCY PREPARATION GUIDE

Preface

Where to start? As I sit to write this, we are facing rising costs and economic trouble all over the world; wars, famine, violence, government shut downs and regime changes, just to name a few. The planet is facing some pretty uncertain times. There isn't a need to panic, but I do believe it is time to prepare... for anything or everything. I am not in a financial position to purchase everything in this guide. I have made a good start, maybe even a great start. The idea is this: buy an item, then another. Shoot, buy three next time. ***Just <u>START</u>!!!***

Don't look at this guide as the end-all and be-all of disaster preparedness. This is NOT a complete list. While I have taken great pains to make it as all-inclusive as I can, it is still going to be missing something. If I knew what it was, I would have put it in.

This guide recommends that you own guns. I firmly believe that firearms are an absolute necessity for being prepared. Think of it this way: you don't know how long the situation will last. You may need to hunt for food. People during disasters are willing to do a lot of things, terrible things, for the good of their family. Would you die for your loved ones? Would you kill to protect them, to keep them from starving? You may not, but someone else might. Having supplies WILL make you a target in a long term catastrophe. Protect yourself. Protect your family. Protect your supplies. That being said, I do not believe that everyone should own a gun. First, check the laws where you live. They differ greatly across this country so that I can't cover them all here.

If you aren't willing or capable of following the rules and laws of safe gun ownership...DO NOT BUY A GUN!!! If you aren't willing or capable of becoming familiar with your weapons... DO NOT BUY A GUN!!! If you aren't willing or capable of practicing with your weapons...DO NOT BUY A GUN!!!

I hope I've made this clear enough. If you have children, you must make them "Gun Safe Kids." They should be allowed to touch, use, look at and shoot them. You must supervise your children whenever they are with your guns. Satisfy their curiosity. Give them your time, every time they ask. Keeping guns and ammo locked up isn't enough. Curious kids will always find a way.

Instructions

So how does this thing work?

Here's the deal. This should be used as a shopping guide and for keeping records of your stores. The "lists" are all double spaced. Use the extra space to add items I missed, notes for the items, to swap an item on the list for one of yours or to replace an expired or broken item. I suggest that you start with the smallest kit (***Every Day Carry, or EDC Kit***); you'll make progress faster and be more motivated to move on to the next list. Copy your lists and place them in or on your kits. I recommend that you laminate these to protect them. With the ***Home Kit***, you can make several copies and place one on each bin. Use them as a check list; either highlight the items that <u>are</u> in that bin or mark out the items that <u>are not</u> with a marker.

Work with a friend or two. A lot of items are cheaper in bulk. Buy two or three and share or sell to a friend. Consider keeping duplicates of some items. A good rule to remember is, "Two is one and one is none." If you break it, do you have another? Having a friend with the same kits and supplies can be priceless in an emergency. If it's a co-worker, you might want to put together a small kit for work. If you and your friends are regularly at the same place, put a kit there. My buddy has the combination to my gun safe. If I can't get home, he can go to my place and retrieve my family and gear for me. My wife has a kit in her car. It contains enough for her and our kids. If we travel together, I bring my car kit with us. My kids have their own kits. These go with them when they travel without us. My kids are eight and thirteen now. It's easier to get them involved than younger kids. Find a way to work it into your life.

TRY YOUR GEAR!!! An emergency is a horrible time to figure it out. This summer, my family is going out with our ***Go Bags*** for three days. Try it. Learn, practice, teach, enjoy… think of it as a great time to develop new skills and share the knowledge you have with others. Eat some of your food storage. Sample a few delicious Mountain House meals. Test your water filtration. Experiment with the Aquamira tablets. Spend one night in a makeshift sleeping arrangement (not your nice, cozy sleeping bag). Do a "Home Test" of your gear too. Friday after work, turn off all power, heat, water, etc. in your house and don't turn it back on until you get ready for work Monday morning. See how you do without the creature comforts for just two days. You might want to power up at bedtime to keep the fridge cold... or not.

This workbook should make shopping for items on the go a bit easier for you. Write in this book in pencil, that way you can make changes later. Have you bought a better set of radios? Erase the old ones and add the new. Used up your batteries? Buy new ones and change the "use by" date on your list. This will give you a living workbook. It can change and grow. As items expire, are upgraded, used, broken, etc., you can just replace that item on your list. Fill out your lists in this book and copy them so you can keep a list in the garage with your gear. Keep a list at the office. Send a buddy to get something from your place and you can tell him what kit it is in. Keep your mind open and your plan flexible. This is the key to survival.

Hope this helps, Todd

EVACUATION AND RETURNING HOME

Get out of Dodge

The faster you can get out, the better your chances of making it. Roads will quickly become congested. Decide how much time you have to get rolling and stick to it.

This is a list of tasks to perform before you leave your home during an evacuation. Do these in order as time allows. If you must leave immediately, do so. It's not worth risking your life. Get your gear, your family, your pets, and GET OUT! Now it's time to start PLAN "B."

- Make sure everyone has their Go-Bag
- Fill water containers to take with you – if possible, bring your water collection system with you. Fill it with supplies.
- Make sure all batteries are charged before you leave (for portable devices)
- Check weapons and ammunition (it's a bad idea to leave these behind)
- Listen to radio or TV if possible for road closures and delays
- Everyone should know the destination AND the route
- Discuss a "Plan C" route and destination in case your secondary location is inaccessible.
- If possible, let your out-of-area contact (OAC) know that you are on the move to your
- secondary location
- Everyone should have the contact and family info pack
- Bring Pet Go-Bags
- Make sure everyone is dressed for the conditions along the way and at the destination
- Secure your valuables before you leave
- Fill bath tub with water and lightly chlorinate
- Bring as much food and water as space will allow
- Bring your Large First Aid Kit (L. FAK)

- Bring as much of your Home Kit as possible
- Fill vehicles with fuel as needed and bring what you can with you.
- Clean and bring your latrine kit and toiletries
- Secure all loose gear
- Check tires and fluids
- Turn off your home utility mains in this order - GAS, *then* WATER, and *then* POWER
- Take a head count. Then do it again
- Take a third look at the supplies you are leaving behind... are you sure you won't need that?
- Go to bed with a full tank of gas, in an emergency, there is always a rush on gas

NOW GET MOVING BEFORE THE GRIDLOCK SETS IN!!!!

They See Me Rollin'

We've covered what to do before you jump in the car and get going. Now let's talk about what to do after you pull out of the driveway. You should have a destination planned well in advance. Really, you should have three destinations. You should have a friend or family member who lives at least a couple hundred miles from you, established as your OAC (Out of Area Contact). Your OAC will be there to leave messages with. Your whole group needs to know how to contact your OAC. Should you become separated or have family converging from other areas, your OAC will be an important part of getting everyone to the *CORRECT* destination. You need a plan in place in the event that your OAC is unreachable.   You should have a list of your destinations in order of importance. #1 on the list is the first place you will head in an emergency. If that location is not safe or inaccessible, move on to location #2.

Keep your eyes open! Hopefully you aren't traveling alone. You'll need one of two things; a rested backup driver to take turns with and /or a good navigator and spotter who can keep an eye and ear out for danger. Listen for news reports about traffic or trouble on your route. Have good maps that cover your entire journey. Highlight alternative routes ahead of time. If you must stop for rest or repairs along the way, keep a person on security detail. Take shifts. It's difficult for trained professionals to remain hyper-alert for more than a few hours at a time. Once you have arrived (hopefully safely and intact) at your destination, leave one person on security while you get unpacked. Get them to a vantage point where they can see trouble coming.

Now that you have arrived at your safe destination, do your best to get a handle on how long you will have to stay there. Is it a week? A month? Is it your new home? Having these answers ahead of time may help you keep your sanity. Listen for news reports if available. Settle in, but don't let your guard down.

The Journey Home

They've sounded the all clear. Now what do you do? Review the list of what to do when you leave home. You should follow the same steps. Fill your water containers, gather food for the trip, charge batteries, check fuel levels, repack your Go-Bags, stow your gear, take care of utilities, check the news and weather, notify your OAC… you know the drill. Gather the family and pets for a last head count and load 'em up. Remember to have your alternate destinations and routes planned. You never know, *your* home or neighborhood may not be safe yet. Gather as much information as possible. Try to call neighbors or friends to get a report on local conditions. Depending on what caused you to hit the road, you may have a longer, more difficult drive home. Be prepared for long waits in traffic. Water, snacks, games and family stories will help you pass the potentially long hours with your sanity intact. Keep an eye out for opportunists; people posing as if stranded but hoping to take advantage of you. This doesn't mean you shouldn't stop to help others, but keep an eye out for trouble and maybe have a family member pull guard duty. Just remember... people do crazy things when there is no danger. Imagine what they would do in a disaster. Stay safe, positive and be prepared.

So, you're in the home stretch. You can see your street ahead. There's a bright ray of sunshine beaming down on your house, beckoning you home. *WAIT!!!* Don't just rush in and jump into a nice hot shower! You have no idea if hooligans are up to shenanigans in your absence! Approach your neighborhood with caution. Look for signs of damage, looters, fire and other emergency vehicles, utility vehicles making repairs. Don't charge in. Get a feel for what's going on and then if it looks safe, proceed to your house. Don't pull straight into the driveway. If possible, get a look at your home. Does it appear the same as when you left? I understand that you exited in a hurry, but does anything look out of place?

If all is well, carefully approach. Do a perimeter walk for three reasons; look for damage (man-made or otherwise), look for signs of intruders and smell for gas leaks. If everything is ok, go on in. If not, notify authorities and leave. City resources are probably stretched thin, so response time will be insane, but it's better to be safe than sorry.

The Returning Home List

- Inspect for structural damage
- Check for downed power lines
- Turn OFF the gas valves for the appliances, water heater and furnace if possible
- Turn ON main gas valve and smell for leaks in and around the home

- Turn on appliance and furnace valves one at a time and light pilots as per manufacturer's instructions - if you don't understand EVERYTHING in the instructions, call a professional.
- Turn on power and check for tripped breakers, as well as GFIC breakers or outlets. This is a good indicator of electrical damage.
- Turn on water and inspect for leaks in and around the home
- Check both cellular and landline phones for service.
- Notify your OAC that you have arrived at your destination

Now that your home is settled, go see if you can help your neighbors. Crisis is the time to draw your community together. Share your knowledge and skills, but keep quiet about your supplies and gear unless you *truly* trust them. If you aren't a little careful here, your home might be the *Motel 6* during the next emergency. Your supplies probably can't support the entire neighborhood. While you're helping outside the home, leave family members to work their way down this list:

- If the situation appears safe – secure your firearms properly
- If water is functioning: fill containers, bath tub (if not already or if not in a Water BOB), and begin filtration – just because the water is on, doesn't mean its safe. Check the news for reports on water quality
- If power is functioning, charge cell phones, radios, batteries, etc...
- Refill fuel if possible and add a preservative
- Listen to radio, TV, or weather band for news or updates to the situation
- Make any repairs that may be necessary to secure your home
- Now that your home is secure, check on neighbors, friends and notify your out of area contact that you are home
- Restock food and filtered water supplies
- Make a list of items used and replace them as soon as possible
- Make a list of items you would have liked to have on hand and add those to your notebook and your kit

Practical Advice

When Should you Leave?- If told to evacuate, you should probably go. You have to look at the potential dangers and the cost/benefit factors of staying or relocating. Can you move enough of your gear to a new location in the given time? Ask yourself, "Is it dangerous to me and my loved ones to stay here or more dangerous to travel?"

What to Do and When- When you first hear of an emergency (radio, TV, word of mouth), assess the potential for widespread panic or disruption of services. How far away is it? How fast can the problem spread or will it at all? Should you rush home or stop for additional supplies? Should you contact family and friends? Is it time to plan or time to act? (The time to plan has already passed.) First, get yourself and your gear ready. Decide to shelter in place or go to your AWAY shelter. Then contact your group and tell them what to get ready. They will look to you for guidance and reassurance. If you are panicking, they will too. Keep calm and follow your plan.

Long Term Storage (LTS)- Long term storage is anything with a shelf life or viable storage life beyond three years. These can include food, water, fire starting materials, fuel, ammunition, medications, first aid kits (FAK) and cleaning or toiletries. Many items are not designed to be stored at all. Look at expiration dates. These will vary greatly how it is stored. For most items, heat is the biggest enemy. Your *Car Kit* will need to have items rotated more often than the things stored in your basement; generally speaking, the cooler the better. Pay attention to storage temperatures and recommendations on the packages.

Rotating of Storage- FIFO... First In, First Out. Get in the habit of using your stores. Buy two cans of beans, then use your oldest can of beans first. When you buy an item, put it at the back of the shelf and use the item in front. This will keep your stock as fresh as possible and give you a chance to try recipes for your stored food. When the markets are closed, it will be quite a shock to go "cold turkey" on your usual menu.

Rioting and Looting- This is a delicate situation for many when discussing the haves and the have-nots. Many people recommend you share the fact that you are preparing with as few people as possible to avoid being a target in an emergency. There were a lot of people hurt or killed in the wake of Hurricane Katrina. People will do terrible things to stay alive or to feed their families. Keep the "signs of life" at your home to a minimum at night. Only run your generator during the day. Keep your blinds closed at night to avoid drawing unwanted attention. I could write a whole book on security procedures, but that is not the point of this guide. Just watch out for the world around you.

How Much Is Enough?- How long do you think the situation will last? How long until services are restored? How long until trucks are rolling and stores are open? That's how much you will need. You might want to get a bit more than that so you will have enough to share should your party grow in size. You may need to provide aid to others. Your kids may have friends over when disaster strikes. Your neighbor (probably unprepared) may decide that you are his savior. Be prepared for guests, just like mom always taught you! Turning people away during a crisis is hard to do. You may need to stock extra supplies for charity or to barter with. Ammunition and shoes will be very valuable in a long term disaster.

Resistance- You will meet with some resistance from family, friends, co-workers and neighbors. Don't worry, when "IT" hits the fan, they'll forgive you. Some will say you are hoarding. Well, hoarding is different than preparing. Hoarding is taking more than you need or more than is your share. Preparing will decrease the likelihood that you will be a burden on already strained resources when a disaster occurs. Some will question your faith in God. *God will care for me* is a terrible excuse for not preparing. My brilliant wife puts it this way, "God didn't flood the earth and ***then*** tell Noah to build a boat!" How many times in your life have you bought something "just in case?" This is exactly like that, but with a goal in mind.

Gardens- Whether you have a green thumb or not, a long term disaster situation will be a serious drain on your food stores. A garden will be irreplaceable in these situations. Visit your local nursery and ask about the fruits and vegetables that grow well in your climate and specifically your area or neighborhood. Ask about classes for beginners or advanced gardeners. The more productive you can make your garden, the better off you will be. If you have a surplus, you may be able to barter for meats or poultry. Consider your water situation and your sun exposure. These will have a drastic effect on your garden's output. You may want to look into trimming or removing trees or branches to get more sunlight or increase your plantable area. You should try to grow fruits, vegetables and herbs. Look at small green houses for your starter plants and herbs. Begin your garden NOW!!! Once disaster has struck, it's too late to start.

S.O.S.- Dot, Dot, Dot, Dash, Dash, Dash, Dot, Dot, Dot. Three short, three long, three short... This is done with a flashlight, banging on something, honking a horn, any way you can. Learn it, memorize it, KNOW IT!!!

DUTIES - SKILLS - COMMUNITY

I honestly believe that my time spent as a Boy Scout set the stage for my love of our Nation, my moral character, preparedness mindset and drive to succeed. I made some lifelong friendships. I learned how to be an individual and a part of a team in the Boy Scouts. I found out that I could dig deep and push through hardship. (The 50 mile pack trip was rough as a kid.) I learned to pack light but be prepared. The things I learned in Boy Scouts are the same things that inspired me to write **Fully Prepped**.

The Boy Scout Oath says it pretty well.

"On my honor I will do my best
To do my duty to God and my country
and to obey the Scout Law;
To help other people at all times;
To keep myself physically strong,
mentally awake, and morally straight."

Physical, mental, moral... You need skills! This section about the Oath explains the things that all citizens should strive for.

The Meaning of the Boy Scout Oath

Before you pledge yourself to any oath or promise, you must know what it means. The paragraphs that follow will help you understand the meaning of the Scout Oath:

On my honor . . .

By giving your word, you are promising to be guided by the ideals of the Scout Oath.

I will do my best . . .

Try hard to live up to the points of the Scout Oath. Measure your achievements against your own high standards and don't be influenced by peer pressure or what other people do.

To do my duty to God . . .

Your family and religious leaders teach you about God and the ways you can serve. You do your duty to God by following the wisdom of those teachings every day and by respecting and defending the rights of others to practice their own beliefs.

and my country . . .

Help keep the United States a strong and fair nation by learning about our system of government and your responsibilities as a citizen and future voter.

America is made up of countless families and communities. When you work to improve your community and your home, you are serving your country. Natural resources are another important part of America's heritage worthy of your efforts to understand, protect and use wisely. What you do can make a real difference.

and to obey the Scout Law; . . .

The twelve points of the Scout Law are guidelines that can lead you toward wise choices. When you obey the Scout Law, other people will respect you for the way you live; and you will respect yourself.

To help other people at all times; . . .

There are many people who need you. Your cheerful smile and helping hand will ease the burden of many who need assistance. By helping out whenever possible, you are doing your part to make this a better world.

To keep myself physically strong, . . .

Take care of your body so that it will serve you well for an entire lifetime. That means eating nutritious foods, getting enough sleep, and exercising regularly to build strength and endurance. It also means avoiding harmful drugs, alcohol, tobacco, and anything else that can harm your health.

mentally awake, . . .

Develop your mind both in the classroom and outside of school. Be curious about everything around you, and work hard to make the most of your abilities. With an inquiring attitude and the willingness to ask questions, you can learn much about the exciting world around you and your role in it.

and morally straight.

To be a person of strong character, your relationships with others should be honest and open. You should respect and defend the rights of all people. Be clean in your speech and actions; and remain faithful in your religious beliefs. The values you practice as a Scout will help you shape a life of virtue and self-reliance."

Excerpted from page 45-46, Boy Scout Handbook, 11th ed, (#33105), copyright 1998 by BSA, ISBN 0-8395-3105-2

and from page 420-421, Webelos Scout Book, 1998 edition, (#33108), copyright 1998 by BSA, ISBN 0-8395-3108-7

Honor

Your word is all you have. Once tarnished it is hard to repair. People judge your worth by your word. Be fair and honest in all that you do.

Effort

A prolonged event will be the hardest thing most people will ever have to endure. It will take everything you have to persevere. Put your best effort into your preparations. Your life will depend on it.

Faith

You better have it! My strength comes from The Lord, period.

"I can do all things through Christ who strengthens me."

Philippians 4:13
New King James Version (NKJV).

The hardest times in my life can all be looked at (in hindsight) as necessary to get me to where I am today. I wouldn't change a thing; it would discredit all the work that God has done in my life. Find your strength. If it isn't in God, find *YOUR* source. Family is a good one. Friends, survival instinct, pure stick-to-itiveness, whatever it is, it better be good. You're going to need more than the promise of tomorrow to strive for.

Country

If you love this Nation, its traditions, founding principles, and Constitution, we need you to help rebuild should a nationwide disaster come to our shores. Be a part of your community NOW! Be active. Find a place to serve. We need you now too. More than ever, we need strong leaders and helpers in our Nation. Evil, corruption, and greed have all but devoured the moral fiber of our great Country. We need people of courage and conviction to be the eyes, ears, and HANDS! We can no longer turn a blind eye. Political correctness has destroyed us. If you are afraid to offend someone who is doing wrong, you are part of the problem. You know right from wrong... STAND UP!

Scout Law

A Scout is:

Trustworthy, Loyal, Helpful,
Friendly, Courteous, Kind,
Obedient, Cheerful, Thrifty,
Brave, Clean, Reverent.

These are the things that make you a citizen. Live up to these principals. These aren't for Scouts. These are for human beings! These are the things that turn houses into neighborhoods and neighborhoods into communities.

Helpful

Are you prepared? Are you more prepared than your friends? Your neighbors? You need to be prepared for the unprepared. They will come. You need a charity stash; items and food there specifically for those who have failed to plan. You are morally obligated to help. However, you are not obligated to starve for their sake. Give them what they NEED and tell them, "This is all I have for you." And send them on their way. Take care of their immediate needs and a little something to give them hope.

Right now is the time for you to decide if you are willing to defend your stores (and survival) from those who would take it by force. Decide now, before you are forced to make this important decision in real time. You will need a plan.

Physically Strong

If you are in terrible shape before disaster, you're going to have a harder time in a prolonged event. Start now - diet, exercise and training are necessary to survive. Take some form of martial art which can serve several purposes. It is great exercise and will improve your balance and flexibility. It teaches honor, discipline and control. Train hard. Post-disaster life will be much harder. Shoot, a month without electricity would be disastrous for most.

Mentally Awake

Learn now! Medical training, vehicle or small motor repair, sewing, canning, shooting, leather work, soap making, cooking, candle making, tactical planning... All of these will be needed in a major disaster. They are terrible skills to learn "on the job." Get them now! You don't need to know everything, just expand in areas you have interest. Add one area you know you are weak in. Add people to your network or group who have the skills that you don't. You don't have to do it alone. Build a team. Make a plan. Play to the strengths in your group. Improve your weakest areas. Cross train with others in your group to create a bit of redundancy.

Morally Straight

If the people around you in a disaster can't trust you, you aren't going to make it. Show yourself to be of good character now. Build a reputation of honesty and good work ethic. After a disaster strikes, it will be too late to fix how you are viewed. Prove your worth. You need to be a valuable part of your family, your group, your neighborhood, and your community. Get involved.

Do you see the value in these principals? Can you see how this will bring us together in times of crisis? Start today. Talk to your neighbors, walk through your neighborhood, get involved in your community.

Skills

Many people are just getting into prepping, whether they're a soccer mom putting back extra groceries or someone who has just become interested in a self reliant lifestyle. A lot of these people believe that all you need to make it is a locker full of guns and ammo and a basement full of food. **This is nearly as dangerous as being totally unprepared!**

Stuff will not save you. Not in a prolonged disaster. Maybe not in a short term emergency either. Skills, knowledge, experience... these are the keys to survival.

Definition of skill (n)
skill[skil]

> ability to do something well: the ability to do something well, usually gained through training or experience

> something requiring training to do well: something that requires training and experience to do well, e.g. an art or trade

> Synonyms: ability, talent, cleverness, dexterity, expertise, proficiency, skillfulness, handiness, knack, aptitude, competence, flair

Cooking, building, repairing, fabricating, crafting, smithing, sewing... these are the skills that not only last a lifetime, but will prevail in hard times.

You have to believe that you will survive. You need the fortitude to continue when your body says "Quit." You need the mettle to carry on when your mind says "Enough is enough!"

Skills are as important, maybe more important, as gear! You need skills to survive. You need skills for barter. You need skills to be a vital part of a surviving community. Many skills can be learned easily and may prove to be beneficial to you beyond your dreams. Some can be learned by reading a book, watching a video, taking weekend seminars; others may be offered at a local community college.

Here are my short descriptions of some of the most important skills in no particular order:

Welding

Learning to stick weld is not that hard. You just need to be proficient enough to know which rods or amp setting to use. You're not going to build a bridge tomorrow. I hope...

Many community colleges offer classes on welding. Once you own a welder, you'll find a million and one uses for it. Not to mention should you ever need some extra cash, you can barter or start your own small welding business.

The small Lincoln boxes are 220V welders that can be picked up pretty cheap in a pawn shop or on Craigslist. These are great for nearly any situation you could find yourself needing a welder; but they require a 220V power source. A better choice would be a portable generator/welder combo. This way you can take your welder with you plus have a self contained unit. Honda, Lincoln and Hobart make excellent combo units. Just stay away from the cheap ones. You really do get what you pay for.

Frugality

Being careful in the use of resources makes good sense. This applies not only to consumables but also to the use of time. Avoiding waste and eliminating expensive habits will result in a simpler life, but a life that is more likely to be productive. You will have finite resources. Use everything. Repurpose as much as possible. Think twice before throwing anything away.

Small Engine Repair

Knowing how to repair your generator motor or other small engine could be crucial. You could either take it into town or call a repair guy. The only problem with this idea is that you may not be able to call anyone. You may not want to call anyone. Your local community college is here to save you. Many have classes on basic and advanced small engine repair. Remember, you may be limited in parts, so stock up on the most likely parts ahead of time. You don't need to know everything, but a basic knowledge and ability will go a long way. So the next time your butterfly stick's closed or you manage to "He-Man" the pull cord loose, you won't be left scratching your head... you'll know how to fix it!

Fishing

No, I'm not talking about grabbing a can of worms and heading off to a stream. I'm talking about throwing down a ton of fish in a hurry. If you live anywhere near a large body of water, such as a lake, river or pond, you need to learn how to catch a lot of fish in as little time possible. Learn how to make fish traps, nets and trotlines. Then learn how to use them properly.

Many fish have seasonal spawns where they will congregate in schools and move en masse to spawning areas. Most everyone knows that Salmon do this, but fish that live in lakes and rivers do this as well. Stripers, Bass and Crappie, as well as many others, spawn this way. You may want to pick the brain of a local fishing guide. He should know what you'll need for your regional species. There are books on the market that will teach you these skills. Be warned, many of these techniques are illegal in a lot of states. Be sure to read the regulations for your area before trying any of these techniques. Of course, in a survival or emergency situation you'll probably be more worried about eating than facing down Barney Fife, the Fish and Game Warden.

Hunting

It's easy to assume that all self reliant families know how to hunt. But that isn't the case. Many don't even have the skills to find and harvest squirrels, let alone a big buck. To be successful on a regular basis, these skills take some time. It's not as easy as going out on your porch and shooting the squirrels your neighbor is feeding. You can bet that when a prolonged disaster strikes, others will be out putting food on the table; food that should be on your table!

Hunting isn't really a YouTube kind of skill. You're going to have to go old school on this one. Your best bet is to find a friend who is successful and tag along. Have them show you what to look for and the signs left by the game in your region. Once you "get a feel" for the forest, how animals move and use the woods, you'll be on the right track to become a good hunter.

Gardening

Whether you simply grow some tomatoes and greens or plant a whole mini-farm on an acre or two, knowing how to grow your own food will allow you to supplement your pantry. Knowing how to harvest seeds from your garden for next season should be high on your list of priorities. Learn to work the land you have so that you can grow fruits and vegetables that will feed your family and possibly provide excess for bartering.

Butchering

This will come in very handy for those of you who wish to raise your own livestock and to take advantage of local critters. You may need to bribe a friend or neighbor who already knows how to do this and convince them to show you as well. Learning how to properly cut up an animal, whether it's a deer, cow or rabbit, is a valuable skill that every person wanting to be self sufficient should learn.

Butchers in my area charge $ .75 cents to $1.00 per pound to kill, butcher and package a steer. If you've got an 800 pound steer, that can add up to a lot of money. I've even heard some butchers charging $2.00 per pound or more to do this! If it is not your cow, it can be a couple dollars up to $10 a pound for good grass fed grass finished beef. Deer typically cost at least $100 and more to have processed. You can save yourself a ton of money and learn to do it yourself!

Trapping

Trapping gives the self sufficient person an additional avenue for procuring fresh meat. Unlike hunting, traps that you set are working for you around the clock. You can also set a lot of traps in order to cover a wide area. You could even set traps in one area and hunt another. It's like having two or more people out getting your food! This increases your chance of catching something for the dinner table.

What's most important is knowing what type of trap to use in order to catch your intended target. If you're wanting to catch a wolf, then you'll be sorely disappointed if you use a trap or snare intended for a squirrel

Hair Cutting

Hey, Sasquatch, how often do you get your hair cut? Once a month? Every two months? When there is no salon or barbershop around the corner, or worse, no money for a salon. The next best thing is a good set of shears and someone with a modicum of hair cutting knowledge. Being even moderately groomed will greatly improve morale in your group. Couple a good haircut with a warm solar shower and you might even feel human again.

To get started in home barbering and haircutting, you need some barber shears and a trimmer. I happen to use a Wahl. A portable trimmer will run off of solar power so the lack of electricity should not be a problem, although there are plenty of battery operated models to choose from as well.

I do suggest that you acquire some basic skills practicing on family and friends so that when the time comes, you can perform basic hair cutting for other members of your survival community. We are lucky enough to have a family member in the business.

Gunsmithing

If you're living the self reliant lifestyle, then chances are good you own some firearms. Can you disassemble, clean and reassemble them (and have them work properly)? Sadly, some believe they can, but their idea of cleaning is spraying a half can of Break-free into the action and calling it clean. Do you have *ANY* spare parts around for your guns? (Extra magazines don't count.) Probably not, but you should and you should learn how to fix a firearm if it breaks. Brownell's has a huge library of videos and books on Gunsmithing. YouTube probably has what you need also. In a grid down situation, you'll most likely be out of luck on the videos. So grab yourself some books that cover your type of guns and learn how to clean and repair them.

Basic Carpentry

Can you frame a wall, build a barn, square a building or plumb a sink? If not, these skills are easily learned. Your local community college may come to your rescue again. If you're the type that can learn from a book, then you can find many fine books on building and carpentry at your local hardware store. These skills are necessary, should we face a long term crisis. Carpentry, electrical and plumbing skills will all be in demand and you could make a lot of friends quickly if you are the one in your area who knows how to fix things. Remember, you probably won't have power. Learn how to do all these things *WITHOUT* all those fancy do-dads you use now. Forget the laser level... learn how to use a plumb bob. You'll also need HAND TOOLS *not* POWER TOOLS. Start hitting the yard and estate sales now!

Sewing

Back in the day, most young ones were taught how to mend clothes, sew on a patch or button and darn socks. These domestic skills were not limited to just the girls; little boys were also taught to sew, iron, hem and darn. In a world where new clothes and even bolts of fabric are precious, if available at all, sewing skills will be needed to create new garments out of old. Things like sanitary pads for the ladies will need to be made from scrap pieces of cloth and washable TP from old rags may be needed. But most of all, clothes will need to be repurposed and made usable again. For that, someone with sewing skills will be invaluable to the community.

Auto Repair

You'll need to learn basic maintenance and repair skills and obtain some advanced skills like being able to rebuild an engine or transmission. If you have a newer computer controlled vehicle, you may be out of luck if parts are not available. Cars don't share many parts these days. Older, non-computer controlled vehicles are much easier to work on than those built today. These older vehicles may also afford some protection from EMP attacks. With no sensitive electronics to be fried in case of an attack, they just may be the hot "new" item in the neighborhood.

Men and women should be able to change a tire, change out starters, alternators, water and fuel pumps. If you can't do these simple chores, you'd better have money or another vehicle to rely upon should one go down.

Entertaining

This tip comes from Gaye Levey, "This skill is something I have rarely, if ever, seen mentioned in prepping circles. In a world where there are no movies, no TV, no video games and no mall, staying pleasantly occupied during leisure periods will be a challenge. The risk, if there is no entertainment, is that you will either work yourself to death because you are bored or you will become depressed due to the lack of imaginative stimulation."

Entertaining in a post SHTF world may include singing or playing the harmonica, guitar or accordion. It might also include teaching a group to dance, play charades or even to play a rousing round of canasta. Knowing how to entertain others and bring a bit of fun into their lives is a special trait that can be honed now and put into use over and over again, regardless of how bad things get." A large collection of board games may also be well worth the expense!

Ham Radio Operation

Ham radio, also known as amateur radio, involves using various types of radio communications equipment to connect with other people who are also ham operators. The "amateur" title just indicates that they do not make any profit from their activities, but ham operation is a well trained skill. Ham radio operators are required to pass a licensing exam that demonstrates his/her understanding of key concepts involved in radio communications. This ensures that the activities of the ham radio operator will not interfere with the operation of other vital communication services that use radio frequencies. Once they pass the licensing exam, ham radio operators are assigned a call sign that is used to provide their transmissions with a unique identity.

After they are licensed, ham radio operators are not required to use any particular type of equipment. They can modify or construct any radio that meets emission standards. Designing new antennas and hand building amateur radio gear requires substantial skill, but it presents an exciting challenge for electronics enthusiasts.

Ham radios can be *extremely important* in emergency scenarios and are the most reliable equipment when other means of communication fail. Most communities encourage people to learn the skill as part of their emergency preparedness plan. I encourage you to obtain the skill for the benefit of your family and your neighborhood! Communication can be vital for understanding what is going on around you and for progress to be made.

Larger Scale Cooking and Baking

When the pioneers traveled across this country in wagon trains, certain individuals were designated "Cookies." These individuals were made famous by their ability to cobble together meals from whatever provisions were available. Cooks, or "Cookies," will be valuable in a post SHTF community. The reason is there will be a lot to do in the community. Having someone who is capable of cooking for your group or community while the rest of you are gathering wood, maintaining security, fixing whatever broke last night, will be priceless. People need to cat and anyone who has the skill to cook, and especially to bake for a crowd, will find a welcome place in the survival community.

Advanced First Aid

Knowing advanced lifesaving first aid skills should be the goal of every person who is prepping for the worst. Common sense dictates that you should know these skills. I'm talking about skills that go above and beyond band aids and ace bandages. It goes without saying that knowing how to administer first aid can save lives. Basic wound care, suturing skills and even a knowledge of herbal remedies could make a difference in whether your loved ones live or die. You should know how to treat major wounds, such as a sucking chest wound, until help can arrive. Could you set a broken bone? How about removing a bullet? It's not like watching old episodes of ER. At some point during a crisis, first aid skills will be needed. If not you, then possibly by a family member or friend will need them. You may be their only hope for surviving. Does your family or group have a designated medic? What happens if they don't make it? Learn some advanced first aid yourself, your "medic" may need YOU!

People Skills

People skills, social skills, communication skills, i.e. interpersonal skills, will dictate your ability to work with others in a positive and productive way. Having strong people skills will be invaluable when it comes to bartering for goods or services or for controlling a potentially deadly situation with reason instead of force.

Perseverance

Perseverance is described as doing something despite difficulty. Hard times or not, this is the skill that will give you the gumption to keep on going. It will allow you to see the bright side and will also motivate those around you to keep plugging along. By choosing to break insurmountable tasks into manageable pieces, you set yourself up for success when others might just give up before even trying. You must *CHOOSE* to persevere because the alternative is unthinkable.

Defense

Whether you choose a knife, a gun or a club, get to know your defensive weapon well so that you can protect what is yours in a safe and sane manner. Train regularly. Your ability to defend yourself, your family and your supplies will make all the difference when potentially faced with hungry and angry mobs.

Below, I've compiled a list of skills I think everyone should know. This is by no means a complete list, because there is always room to learn more; and the more you know, the greater your chances of survival. But this will give you a solid foundation and a far broader skill set than most people. Having just a basic knowledge in these skills would be immensely valuable.

Skills Everyone Should Have:

- Build a garden
- Drive a stick shift
- Swim
- Start a fire without matches or a lighter
- Use herbal remedies
- Produce beer/wine
- Tan leather
- Cure/smoke meat
- Make soap
- Moderate first aid skills
- Construct animal/fish traps
- Make activated charcoal
- Properly load a backpack
- Conduct basic repairs (auto, equipment, etc.)
- Operate a ham radio
- Defend yourself without a weapon
- Identify surveillance
- Build a rainwater collection system
- Weld
- Archery
- Dehydrate food
- Construct snowshoes
- Avoid and survive hypothermia
- Build a raft
- Navigate using the stars
- Right an overturned raft
- Carpentry skills
- Build with stone/brick (basic masonry)
- Grow a garden from seeds
- Cut down a tree with an ax
- Forage for food
- Sew and/or make clothing
- Pilot a boat
- Shoot a firearm accurately
- Find water
- Ammo reload
- Utilize camouflage

- Construct a pond
- Canning food
- Snow Ski
- Dig a latrine
- Determine authenticity of gold and silver
- Hunt with a Bow
- Rappel
- Follow a trail/tracking
- Use less-lethal weapons (baton, stun gun, pepper spray, etc.)
- Metal working (blacksmith)
- Lose a tail
- Identify and treat for shock
- Operate power tools
- Construct a splint
- Open a can without a can opener
- Drive a motorcycle
- Construct a net
- Identify animals by tracks and scat
- Patch a tire
- Reload ammunition
- Build a bow and arrow
- Administer first aid
- Identify venomous snakes
- Accurately fire a slingshot
- Make candles
- Raise fish (for food)
- Distill water/alcohol
- Hot wire a car
- Cook without a stove
- Survive heat injuries
- Raise livestock
- Find tinder
- Create fertile soil
- Make charcloth
- Properly store food
- Survive a riot
- Sharpen a knife
- Butcher livestock

- Travel without leaving a digital footprint
- Purify water
- Make leather products (sheathes, holsters, boots, etc.)
- Hunt and fish
- Cast bullets
- Maintain a bee hive
- Use hand tools
- Tie several kinds of knots

Working on skills can provide a much needed break from the constant quest to acquire food, gear and supplies. Take the time to think through the personality traits that will help guarantee your survival. In doing so, you will come to realize your self-worth. You are a talented individual with the stuff *AND* skills to survive. Keep in mind, though, that as with any list, this is only a start. With a little time invested, many more skills can be added. How about you... What skills do you have that are on this list? What skills do you think are missing?

Skills, skills, skills... it is sort of like location, location, location. It really is EVERYTHING. Without skills, we are doomed to fail. If you invite someone to be accepted into your home or community, it is going to require some tough scrutiny. Part of that scrutiny will be to evaluate whether they have a useful and needed skill to bring to the group. And by useful skill, I mean a skill that will enhance the lives and lessen the burden of the others that are already there. Goods and gear will have some value, but they are finite and perishable. Skills make you a value to the group as a whole. The more skills you have, the more valuable you will be. After all, if you need to clear out with simply your bug out bag and the clothes on your back, you may be the one knocking on a stranger's door with nothing but your skills to offer. There are two schools of thought on this. In a short to medium term disaster, your skills can save you and your family. Maybe they will put some food on the table. In a long term disaster, your skills will still save your family, but they will also be used to rebuild your neighborhood, your city and our nation. We need to become a nation of "DOers" again. Our parents had some of that. Our grandparents had it oozing out of their pores. Their parents didn't have a choice. You either "did it" or you didn't survive. We live a disposable lifestyle. We have become dependent on replacing things instead of fixing them. We buy things that "do it" for us. *We need to become a nation of "DOers" again!* We won't make it otherwise.

SURVIVAL MUSTS

Make a master list of all of the items you need, have or want for each of these categories.

- Wants/Needs
- Water
- Cooking/Canning
- Food Storage
- Medical
- Personal
- Chem/Nuke/Bio
- Hygiene/Sanitation
- Garden
- Communications
- Vehicles/Transportation/Fuel
- Field gear/Survival
- Clothing/Cold weather gear
- NVG/Optics and Observation.
- Hunting/Trapping/Fishing
- Firefighting
- Tactical/Security
- Tools
- Power/Batteries/Lighting
- Sundries
- Books/Reference materials
- Charity/Barter

EDC Kit

What You Have Is All You Get

Sometimes you end up alone and all you have is what's in your pockets. When you find yourself in such a situation, the equipment or items that you left in the vehicle or back at home are useless to you. They might as well not even exist other than to motivate you to get to them. There are items that you will need should disaster strike. The simple solution to making sure that you have all the items you need is to make a habit of carrying these items every day and everywhere you go. We refer to these items as an everyday carry or EDC kit. The plan is to use an EDC kit to either get you home (either to stay or get your BOB) or to get you to your car (and the CAR KIT). By having a layered approach, you cover more contingencies without lugging your BOB on your back 24/7. I regularly carry a small EDC *bag* with a few useful everyday items. Inside the bag is my EDC *kit*. Should I need to ditch my *bag*, my EDC *kit* is easy to grab out and stuff in a pocket or clip to a belt loop. (Yes, that was a tip...put a carabineer on it!)

Here's a quick list of some suggested items.

- Waterproof Pouch
- Leatherman Squirt Multi Tool
- AAA LED Flashlight
- Space Blanket or similar
- Pocket Knife
- Whistle/Matches/Compass/ Combo
- Paracord 550lb Test
- Small Roll Duct Tape
- Gerber Shard or Artifact
- P-51 Can Opener
- Scalpel Blades
- Super Glue
- Small First Aid Kit
- Ziplock Sandwich Bag
- Water Purification Tablets
- Mini Sharpie or Pencil and Paper
- Small Carabiners
- Latex/Nitrile Gloves
- Cable Saw/Snare Kit
- Cash and Coins
- Non Lube Condom (to store water)
- 1/3 Hacksaw Blade
- Signal Mirror
- Small Zip Ties

Car Kit

You practically live here!

For those that work full time, or even parents with kids, it seems like we spend more time in the car than we do sleeping. It is this exact reason that I recommend the Car Kit. This kit should have enough supplies for your whole family (or maximum occupancy of the car) for 24 hours. The purpose of this kit is to get you home to the rest of your gear. Should you be unable to get home, you'll have the supplies you need to reach another safe location. Though not listed in any particular kit, security and protection should be a part of your preparedness 24/7.

Your Car Kit should cover these categories:

Water

A means to gather, transport, and purify

Food

Prepackaged and long shelf life bars are great

Shelter *(you never know)*

A method of closing off a broken car window as well as making shelter away from you vehicle, a change of socks and a couple blankets could be priceless in winter conditions

Fire

At least three methods of starting it and a way to cut small limbs if necessary

First Aid

You should keep a Medium FAK (M.FAK) in your car at all times

Signaling

Signal mirror, orange flagging, pen and paper, road flares

Light

Long runtime LED flashlight with spare batteries and glow sticks

Navigation

Regional map, compass, GPS, and spare batteries

Bug Out Bags

Who, what, when, why, and where

Why do I need one?

Whether you are planning for a massive financial collapse, an EMP strike, a tornado or the Zombie Apocalypse (or Zombie "Alpacalips" for our Facebook fans), the ability to evacuate or Bug Out quickly will help keep you alive. Are you planning for something or everything? It makes a difference.

How much weight can I carry?

You know your body. How much weight can you carry while hiking for three days? It's not a walk in the park. You may be climbing over debris, avoiding looters or navigating through steep terrain. Be honest with yourself and don't over pack. Depending on what you decide, your Bug Out Bag (BOB) could weigh between 20 and 50 pounds.

How far can I carry it?

How far do you think you can travel, on foot, in three days? What is your terrain like? Weather will play a factor too. Can you carry enough stuff to make it to safety?

How far will I have to go?

Where are you headed? Just out of harm's way? Out of town? Out of state? You need to have predetermined destinations and routes. You need to contact family and friends to let them know where you're headed. Could you make it on foot or will safety be a car ride away?

What size pack actually fits me?

Do you know where a pack is supposed to sit on your body? A standard backpack with proper straps should make the weight of the backpack bear on your hips not on your shoulders. It should fit from your T-shirt collar to your hip bones. It should have a waist strap and a pectoral/chest strap. This will make your pack feel as light as possible.

Where should I keep it?

This is a pretty important question. Do you keep it at home? How about in your car? Maybe at work? I can't answer this for you, but I can help a little. I have a small EDC (Every Day Carry) kit that I keep with me. It is designed to get me to my car. I have a car kit designed to get me home. I have a GoBag designed to get me out of Dodge (G.O.O.D.). In a pinch, I can use my EDC and my Car Kit as a GoBag. I'd be missing a few things, but I wouldn't be totally out of luck. Technically, I would be short on food and water. Except I always have water in the car; and I usually have some food in the car or at work with me. So I could quickly gather what I need. This may seem like a lot of gear... it really is. You don't have to do it all at once. Build an EDC... Then build a GoBag... Then later you can build a Car Kit to fill in the gaps. The idea is that if you and your EDC kit can get to the car and its kit, you have a better chance of getting home to your GoBag. Then you'd have plenty of gear to evacuate with. If you had to abandon the car later, you'd have everything you needed to go on foot.

Now that we've answered all the questions.... let's meet the team!

Please allow me to introduce BOB. Everyone say "Hi BOB!" BOB is your new best friend. He's the one you can count on when disaster strikes, especially if you are evacuated. BOB or Bug Out Bag, Bail Out Bag, GoBag, 72 hour bag, whatever you call it, is your lifeline in an emergency. It is designed to do several things: provide food, shelter and warmth should a disaster happen and you need to leave home. It can give you the tools you need to get from point A to point B should you need to relocate during a disaster. Compact, durable and efficient, these should be the qualities to look for in your BOB items.

These are the categories you'll be dealing with:

- Food
- Water
- Fire
- Shelter
- Rescue
- First Aid
- Weapons
- Other Tools & Necessities

Each of these is crucial. I have a huge list of BOB items. You don't need ALL of them. You need to decide what to carry based on:

- Your skills
- Your physical ability/health
- Your stature (pack size)
- Your climate
- Your family size (adults/children)

If you are not in great physical condition, don't plan on carrying an 80 pound BOB very far. So decide how much you can carry and tailor your kit to match your ability.

Finally….. Gear!!!

This is my favorite part of prepping; not necessarily gadgets, but good old fashioned hardware. Don't get me wrong, I like the gadgets too. I just hate to rely on high tech toys. Some are crucial but most are just designed to replace a skill. *Skills don't break and knowledge weighs nothing.* Don't be dependent on fancy doodads and 95% of this gear is worthless if you don't know how to use it. Some of it is unnecessary if you have the right skills.

Here it goes. Pick and choose whatever you feel YOU need.

Food

- 2400 calorie meal bars
- Trail mix
- Pre-packaged (water, heat and eat)
- Meals like Mountain house or Thrive
- Hard candies (for morale)
- Stainless Camp Cup
- CRKT Eat 'N Tool
- Mini Stove and fuel or grill (Grilliput-grill)
- Snare kit
- Fishing kit

Water

- Water filter
- Aquamira tabs
- Aqua Blox water
- 1 liter wide mouth bottle
- Collapsible water container or
- hydration bladder for pack

Fire

- Bic Lighter
- FireSteel
- Waterproof matches
- Tinder
- Mini hand sanitizer
- Emergency candle

Shelter

- Tube tent, tarp, or backpackers tent
- 2 large garbage bags
- Paracord and knot tying chart
- Bungee cords
- Rescue blanket
- Lightweight bivy bag
- Lightweight sleeping bag
- Plastic drop cloth

Rescue

- Howler whistle
- Signal mirror
- FRS radios
- Crank AM/FM/Weather radio
- Glow Sticks
- Sharpie, pencil, and notepad
- Orange flagging
- Small GPS
- 10x Monocular
- Survival Guide
- Sighting Compass and guide
- Regional map

First Aid

- Small/Medium size first aid kit
- Extra prescription meds if taken
- Basic Essential Oils
- Suture kit and guide
- Latex/Nitrile gloves
- Superglue
- Quick clot or Celox
- Combat gauze
- Tourniquet
- Butterfly/wound closure bandages

- Small surgery kit
- Dental care kit
- Anti-bacterial Soap
- Wet-Wipes

Weapons

CHECK LOCAL LAWS FIRST

- Hand gun (whatever you are-comfortable with) ammo, holster
- Small or Collapsible Rifle (10/22 -takedown or AR-7 type) and ammo
- Machete/Hatchet
- Pocket knife
- Fixed blade knife
- Blunt instruments, clubs, walking stick
- Pepper spray/Bear Spray

Other Tools and Necessities

- Duct tape
- Full Sized Multitool
- Long run LED flashlight
- LEDHeadlamp or strap for LED light
- Batteries for all electronics (X2)
- Baling wire
- Travel toilet paper or tissue pack
- Feminine hygiene product (if needed)
- Rain gear
- Socks/hat/thermal shirt/gloves
- Sunglasses
- N95 particulate mask
- Mosquito headnet
- Zip-Ties
- Small Carabiners
- Small Knife Sharpener
- Sewing kit
- Small prybar
- Folding Saw (with blades for wood/-metal/ plastic)
- Handcuff key (just in case)

- 2 sq ft of Aluminum Foil
- Waterproof bags / Dry Sacks
- Wide brim hat
- Folding shovel
- Hand warmer packets
- Extra prescription glasses
- Tablet washcloth
- Family info and contact kit
- Go Towel (shower in a bag)

Organization

Now that we've talked about what to put in your BOB, I hope it didn't overwhelm you. I really hope you don't try to pack ALL of that in one bag. Speaking of packing, how exactly do we get this stuff into a backpack and not have to dump it out like Granny looking for a mint in her purse?

I use one liter, wide mouth water bottles for most of my kit; five of them to be exact. A red one for first aid, a blue one for water supplies, a green one for cooking tools, a yellow one for rescue gear and a black one to protect my fire starting goodies. I have a dry sack for my clothing items. I use a dry sack for my food as well. That way if I'm in bear or scavenger country, I can hang my food out of reach of the critters easily. Your tools should go in their own compartment of the pack so as to not damage anything else. Your fixed blade knife should go on your pack where it is easily accessible. Mine is on the left shoulder strap. You should have the flashlight or headlamp in an easy to grab location as well. If night sets in, while you're still traveling or setting up camp, you don't want to have to fumble around for it.

I can't tell you what your pack should look like. Pick one with several compartments and some organizer pouches. Decide on a design that works for you. Depending on your physical restrictions and personal skill set, you will need a pack between 2000 and 3000 cubic inches (roughly 30-50 liters). I suggest you get the gear first and then stack it all together. This can give you an idea of the pack size you will need. Try to buy it locally or from a place that takes returns. You don't want to be stuck with a pack you can't use. You'll probably just end up buying the largest capacity for your body size. If you are 5'2" and 100 pounds, don't buy a 60 liter pack. You'll hate yourself. Not that you couldn't carry the weight, but it won't fit your torso correctly. If you are not capable of carrying a pack for long distances, you may need to find one with wheels. Another small word of advice: don't pick a pack covered in bright colors and don't choose a pack that screams "*I HAVE EVERYTHING YOU NEED*" to every passerby. In a true disaster, bad people get worse. Don't be a victim of envy. Also, buy a rain cover for your bag. It's cheap insurance.

Do some research. Find gear that is of quality build. Find gear that is compact. Find gear that fits you. Find gear that helps improve *YOUR* skills. It is very rare for me to endorse a particular item. I do have recommendations for some items, but there are too many products and too many personal opinions for me to tell YOU what you need. If you're stuck on an item or category, email me or catch me on the Facebook page. I'll be glad to help.

Alright! You've answered the questions about "Bugging Out." You've searched the interwebs for all the gear YOU need. You've traversed the hills and valleys (using your new found map and compass skills) for the perfect pack. Somehow you've managed to get all those goodies in Santa's Sack O' Survival. Now what? Do you toss it in a closet to get eaten by moths? Stuff it in the trunk next to last week's gym shorts? I know! You go hide it in the back of the supply closet at work! Yeah! That's the perfect spot!!! *NO! You get off your duff and head out to the "Outernet" and try this stuff out!*

Play (practice) with the items in your kit; get familiar with them. It sucks trying to learn how to start a fire when it's dark and rainy. Try the food. It won't be gourmet, but having an idea what to expect, you may decide to find alternatives due to taste, allergies or size/weight restrictions. Don't just buy gear and expect it to work. Test it!!! If you REALLY need this kit, you are going to be in a pretty crappy situation. This kit is to help you make the best of it. It is not the time to learn; it is the time to apply your skills to the tools at hand. Learn those skills in a safe setting. Learn them now! Try the water filter. Build a fire five different ways. Chop your own firewood. Navigate a 1/2 mile out and back (in the daylight and use the orange flagging to mark your trail... you know, *just in case*). Don't let a disaster be a trial by fire. Plan for the worst and hope for the best. Remember, skills don't break and knowledge weighs nothing!

Duh! I Should Know Better...

Yeah, I screwed up. Shhh! Don't tell anyone! You'll ruin my *DIS*reputation! I am here to help you avoid some mistakes. I can't save you from all of them. I do hope I can save you time and money by learning from my mistakes.

Rule # 1
Heat kills

Your gear has a usable temperature range. Food spoils faster at higher temperatures. Band aids get slimy in a summer car trunk. Medications lose their potency when toasted. We all know the car gets hot in the sun. If you keep your bag in the trunk, you'll have to rotate your perishables and adhesive items more frequently. If you keep it in the closet with the electric water heater... yeah, it's not much better.

Rule #2
Water is our best friend and worst enemy

Mold sucks. Period. Keep your gear away from moisture. I lost an entire travel trailer to mold. A winter storm came through and destroyed thousands of trees in our area. We had a medium sized branch fall on our Get Out Of Dodge trailer. I didn't notice the quarter sized hole in the roof until spring. It looked like a science experiment in there.

Rule # 3
Just because it was expensive doesn't mean it won't break

I'm a hard use kinda guy. I treat most things really well. I can't afford to replace things all the time. That being said, I do get lazy. The screwdriver says "not a pry bar" for a reason. Does that stop me? NAH!

Try not to abuse your gear. You may really need it... five minutes after breaking it, doing something stupid. Tools have an intended purpose. Only use them for what they are designed to do. I broke a really nice drill because the back worked just like a hammer, once; but not twice.

Rule # 4
Imitation is NOT the highest form of flattery

The tool that looks just like the one you want but at 1/2 the price is probably not the tool you want. Cheap knock offs are taking over nearly every facet of our lives. Don't get fooled. I bought a compass that I thought was EXACTLY the same as the Brunton 8040... Nope. Fell apart, IN MY PACK!

Rule # 5
Nothing is Idiot Proof!

Just because it looks really simple to operate does *NOT* mean you should throw out the instructions. There are too many examples to list.

Rule # 6
If it ain't broke, don't try... too often

You should have some idea of the durability of your gear. It should ALWAYS hold up to normal use. Good gear can even handle occasional abuse. Try your gear and make sure it is up to the intended task, but don't go overboard. I had a pretty nice hammer/demolition tool that we jokingly called my *Zombie Apocalypse Hammer*. I showed it off to everyone I could find. I hit this, twisted that and pryed the other thing. Guess what? After repeated abuse... that piece of junk broke in two. Stupid tool!

A Bug Out Bag is one of the most crucial things to have in your preparedness arsenal. I hope this has helped to take the anxiety out of building yours. Good luck!

Water

The average adult uses over 140 gallons of water each day for drinking, bathing, laundry, dishes and watering lawns etc... According to FEMA (Federal Emergency Management Agency), in case of an emergency you should store at least one gallon of water per person, per day and have at least a three-day supply. However, individual water needs vary depending on age, physical condition, activity and climate. Children and nursing mothers need more water and high temperatures can double the water needed. If you have pets, allow a gallon per day for each dog or cat. This is pretty much the minimum for drinking and very water conservative cooking. The Center for Disease Control receives over 4,000 cases each year of illness due to drinking contaminated water. Contaminated water can cause such diseases as dysentery, typhoid and hepatitis.

The Rule of Threes

The average person can survive 3 minutes without air, 3 days without water, and 3 weeks without food. So, right behind breathing, water is important to our survival. Our bodies are made up of roughly 65% water, so we really need to replace what we use through daily life.

So, where do we get water?

Well, Bear Grylls has his way.... *Yuck*. (Although, in extreme situations, I'd do it.)

Municipal Water System

Almost everyone relies on this source. It is already treated and usually filtered down to 0.3-0.4 microns to remove most of the contaminants. It requires functioning infrastructure, maintenance personnel, treatment supplies, pumps and electricity.

A lot of systems have generator backup power that will keep it flowing for awhile after power outage. Pipeline contamination is a possibility with major disasters. Do you know where your town's water source is located (storage tanks and source)? You are dependent on this system for survival unless you plan and prepare ahead of time.

Well Water

A well requires a pump and electricity. Electricity can be from an alternative source like solar, battery bank or generator, if you modify it for multiple power sources. A manual pump could be a solution, and is advisable if your plumbing and well pipe will allow. Ask a well company about options for your system. Rope and bucket set up is possible depending on well diameter. The depth of your well needs to be considered also.

If you don't already have a well, get an estimate of the cost of drilling and implementation as well as what it will take for water to be pumped up to a storage vessel. Find out what size storage is allowed locally and what size fits your property. You will need gravity feed from your storage vessel for emergencies (store higher than user location).

You may need filtration or treatment for drinking, depending on source quality. A well is the best overall self-reliant method, with appropriate backups for power.

Local Lakes, Rivers, Streams, Ponds

First and foremost, transportation of water to your intended location will be of primary concern. Remember, water weighs 8.4 pounds/gallon, so you will need buckets, pails, lids and/or water jugs. Manual transportation will be your only long term option. You may not have fuel or reliable motorized transportation available. Look at a wagon, 2-wheel dolly, hand-truck or bicycle/trailer/ saddlebag set up as possible solutions. A system of pipes with a pump might work if water is near your location. Look for a water source above your location as a gravity system could be implemented. You can store water in vessels at your intended location. Water may need filtration and purification for drinking depending on the source.

Ditch, Gully, Puddle

This is any temporary water source after rainfall, water from runoff in low lying areas, a seasonal creak or drainage. This will probably be much dirtier and filtration and purification are definitely needed for drinking.

Yellow Snow

Here we are at the Bear Grylls solution. Technically your body has already "filtered" this source. In times of dire need, urine is a viable short term solution.

Hot Water Tank

An easy emergency water source that is often overlooked, home hot water tanks usually hold 40 to 50 gallons that should be safe to drink unless it has been sitting unused for a long time. If you are unsure how long it has been sitting, purification is recommended. Water should be fine for a couple months. Most water heaters have a hose spigot for drainage, making it very convenient in a disaster.

Swimming Pool

Depending on the sanitation system used, this source should be for emergency use only if you have questions regarding chemicals. That being said, kids gulp pool water while swimming and survive. Recreational swimming pools are kept to less than 3ppm chlorine, which is safe for drinking. Sunlight and time will quickly deplete the chlorine in an untreated pool. Filtration and purification are recommended but not always necessary, but better to be safe than sorry. Be careful as some pools use a salt based chlorination system and may have salt levels between 2 and 4 parts per million. Fine for cooking but might not be ideal for drinking. A water still or desalinization unit would be handy here.

Use Google Earth to discover who has pools in your area.

Toilet Holding Tank

THIS IS THE TANK, NOT THE BOWL.... *Yuck*! Most toilets hold about two gallons of water in the holding tank. I would recommend purification if used for drinking.

Retail Bottled Water

These allow easy storage of manageable sizes that are very portable. It makes counting "quantity on hand" simple, and most are a good size for hiking or bugging out in backpack. They are clean, air tight containers and should be good for 3-5 years. Keep out of sunlight and avoid UV light. Use a sheet or towel to cover clear bottles.

Home Storage Containment

Purpose built water storage vessels, ranging from five gallons up to several thousand gallons, can be created. They need to be food grade and designed for water storage. These can be portable sizes or in ground/above ground storage tanks. This is the easiest way to achieve the recommendations of 1 to 3 gallons per person, per day. If possible, keep storage out of sun and heat.

Water BOB

This is a clever set-up. It is a 100gal clear plastic bag with a fill spout and a hand siphon pump that fits in your bath tub. At the first sign of trouble, simply lay this out in your bath tub and fill it up. It's that easy. Draining isn't quite as easy. A Shop Vac should do the trick. Remember to treat the water with a small amount of bleach if you leave it filled for more than a few days. It is an air tight system and should give you drinking water for quite a while. The average five foot bath tub holds 30-50 gallons. Jacuzzi type tubs can hold 100 gallons or more.

Rainwater Collection Barrels

Fiskars makes a great rainwater collection system. While not the cheapest way to go, it is very effective and a 58gal system can be found for well under $200. If you only plan to use rain water for watering and cleaning, you could buy the Fiskars downspout diverter and modify a garbage can for collection. You can build your own system from easy to find plans also. Either way, its free water from the sky and your roof is a massive collection area. Get a couple systems if you can. There are other companies that offer these systems or find some info and cobble together your own system. Just be sure you use clean components and glue that is suitable for potable water systems. No sense in saving water if you are going to contaminate it. Filter all drinking and cooking water from this system.

Filtration Methods

Sawyer Point One

This is an amazing filtration system. It is a 0.1 micron system. That's excellent for a filter of any size and these are small. They make a gravity feed system that will treat up to 540 gallons a day. These things have a million gallon guarantee and are field cleanable. Just back-flush the filter with clean filtered water and you're ready to go! Sawyer now makes two smaller units designed for those on the go. Perfect for a Bug Out Bag or just for hiking. Look for the Sawyer Squeeze (smallest system); it is ingenious, or the Sawyer bottle system (comes with its own sport bottle).

Katadyn and Berkey are other traditional water filter systems. These are tried and true systems that work great. They do require replacement filters, so stock up!

Makeshift Filtration

If you are stuck unprepared or otherwise filterless, this is your redneck filter system. This won't be perfect but it really beats having nothing. You will need about an inch of each layer of components.

Here is what you'll need and assemble it in this order with the funnel or bottle "small end down":

- A large funnel or top 1/2 of 2 liter bottle
- A coffee filter or tight knit cloth
- Fine sand
- Crushed fire charcoal (from burnt wood)
- Coarse sand
- Small gravel

Carefully place the fine sand into the coffee filter or cloth so that it doesn't fall through. Place each layer on top and gently shake the bottle to level and compact each layer. Run one gallon of water through this before saving/drinking (to wash the impurities and settle the components). Pour slowly so as to not disturb the layers. Use this to fill a clean container to drink from.

Bleach

Here are instructions for treating water with bleach:

Clear Water: 1 quart – 3 drops, 1 gallon – 1/8 teaspoon, 10 gallons – 1 teaspoon
Cloudy Water: 1 quart – 5 drops, 1 gallon – ¼ teaspoon, 10 gallons – 2 teaspoons
Stir or shake for 1 minute, let stand for 30 minutes.

Pool Shock*

Pool shock, also known as Granular Calcium Hypochlorite, has an indefinite shelf life. It is very concentrated and fairly lightweight.

To make a stock of chlorine solution, dissolve one heaping teaspoon (about one-quarter of an ounce) of high-test (78%) granular calcium hypochlorite for each two gallons (eight liters) of water. To disinfect water add one part of the chlorine solution to 100 parts water to be treated.

Disclaimer: Do your own research for conclusions before using Calcium Hypochlorite.

*This will make a useable dilution that is NOT FOR DRINKING. It will be diluted again to make drinking water.

Iodine Tincture

This is an iodine based solution, usually in liquid form. It is extremely compact and lightweight:

- 5 drops per quart.
- 20 drops per gallon.

Shake and wait 30 minutes before drinking.

This is a quick simple method for hikers. It is not advisable to use this method for more than a few days in a row. P.S. this tastes less than appealing but will keep you alive.

UV light

Use a clear plastic water bottle, two liters or less.

Put in direct sunlight for 6 hours (clear water) or several days if the sun is behind clouds.

This method will kill 90% of all living contaminants. Other similar methods are UV-pen and other portable UV methods, but these require batteries. The most recommended version of these is called the Steri-Pen.

Purification Tablets

These are the lightest and most compact form of purification. It usually takes one or two tablets per quart. Follow instructions on package as each brand differs.

For example: Aquamira Tablets - Remove from foil and place tablet in one liter (34oz) of contaminated water. Allow to sit out of direct sunlight (in your pack, etc...) for four (4) hours to completely treat water.

This is a great solution for treating water overnight. Bad news here is they leave a funny taste. Good news is that they are extremely small. Pre-filter your water through a coffee filter or tight knit cloth for best results. These are great for hikers and Go Bags. Like Iodine, this tastes a bit odd, but it is still water.

Potassium Permanganate

This is another cheap and easy way to purify water. Potassium permanganate crystals can be bought from any chemist and you need add only about 3 or 4 crystals per liter of water (or until the water stains a light pink) and leave for 30 minutes. Potassium permanganate can also be used as a disinfectant for cleaning wounds by adding crystals one by one until water turns purple (approx. 0.01% solution).

If you have a small vial of it and need to purify water, put a few crystals in the water and after a while it is drinkable, a few more crystals in the water and it becomes an antiseptic for wounds, a few more crystals and it can be used to mark a purple SOS in the snow. If you put a few drops of antifreeze from your car, or glycerin from your first aid kit, on some potassium permanganate crystals, you will get fire. This chemical has more than one survival use. The brand Pot Perm is available at Home Depot, Sears, Amazon and a lot of aquarium stores. Look for crystals, not the liquid.

There are better ways to purify water. There are better antiseptics on the market. There are also much better fire starters out there. That being said, a little potassium permanganate goes a long way and has many uses.

Water Still

This fuel hogging method will purify any water (including salt water) into pure water. Water is boiled to steam that is routed through tubing; the steam being condensed back to water. Generally, copper tubing is used as it cools quickly to aid in condensing steam back to water with a minimum of tubing. A method of boiling is required as well as a plentiful fuel source. A 'Still' needs assembly and adaptation to boiler. This is most feasible if added onto a cooking or heating stove.

Boiling

Arguably the safest, non-chemical purification method (along with the Water Still), once the water reaches a rolling boil (212° F, 100° C), it has become safe to drink.

Other options are:

160° F (70° C) for 30 minutes to reach pasteurization
185° F (85° C) for several minutes
Conserve fuel, don't boil longer than necessary.

As with all prepping, do your due-diligence regarding choosing methods of water purification. You should have at least three ways to purify water. Store as much water as you can. If you have a viable year round source of water (that is not grid dependent), you can get away with having less water on hand.

Storage Tips

Thoroughly washed, plastic containers (soda bottles or other water bottles) are good; but glass containers are best. Do not use juice or milk containers as they are difficult to get clean enough for long term storage. Fill the container to the top with regular tap water. If the tap water has been commercially treated from a water utility with chlorine, you do not need to add anything else to the water to keep it clean. If the water you are using comes from a well or water source that is not treated with chlorine, add the appropriate amount of non-scented liquid household chlorine bleach to the water. Tightly close the container using the original cap. Be careful not to contaminate the cap by touching the inside of it with your finger. Place a date on the outside of the container so that you know when you filled it and then store it in a cool, dark place. Replace the water every year, if not using commercially bottled water.

Water Purification

Personally, I believe the Sawyer filter is the best option but in the absence of a good water filtration system, use coffee filters, paper towels, cheese cloth, or cotton balls at the bottom of a funnel to filter cloudy or dirty water before boiling or adding bleach. It is a good idea to do this to all water before putting it through a regular filter. This filters out the larger particles that clog a filter the fastest. In a disaster, never assume that your tap water is safe for more than the first day or two. If there is any hiccup or disruption of water from your tap, filter everything after that. Filter or purify all drinking and cooking water.

Food Storage

FIFO, not *FIDO*... That's dog food storage. This is FIFO (First In First Out). This is the general rule for food storage. When you buy a new can of soup, put it at the back of the shelf, that way the next can you use is older. There are some great shelf systems made just for this. There are also good plans available to make your own. The prefab ones are pricey. They also make some smaller units that you just place on your existing shelves. These are made for soup can size or the big #10 cans. It's always best to label cans with a purchase date. Use a Sharpie or paint pen to clearly label all of your food stock; the same goes for your frozen foods and dry storage foods. Keep food as cool as possible. A basement, low in a closet or away from a water heater or heater, is ideal. Higher cabinets will be subject to warmer temperatures. Keep storage foods away from your refrigerator and freezer... They are only cold on the inside. The outside can be over 90 degrees! The closer to 60 degrees you keep your food storage, the better. For example, an MRE (Meal Ready to Eat) can be stored for about two years at 100 degrees. It can be stored for almost eleven years at 60 degrees. This is true for most foods. The lower the temp, the longer it stays fresh.

This has got to be the easiest part of preparedness to get started. Do you buy groceries? Good, you know how to shop. Can you spot the difference between cheap and bargain? Cheap is just as the word says... cheap: cheap price, cheap quality, cheap quantity, cheapskate. Don't do that to yourself. Bargain is a better word for what you are looking for; quality goods at a fair price or less. Next time you go shopping, buy a couple extra cans of veggies. There, now you are started. Do that every time you shop. That's how it's done. If your budget is tight, find small cuts to make, but make a bunch of them. A couple bucks here and there can make the difference. Find a local discounter or "dented can store." These have been on their way out over the years, but they are still around. Clip coupons, chase sales, change stores, whatever it takes to save a dime. Nowadays it's best to go to a warehouse store and buy rice, beans, pasta, oats, etc.... Check online for deals on bulk goods. Restaurant supply stores are another great resource for larger quantities. Have you heard of Sysco or US Foods? Get your group together and come up with a budget you can maintain and plan a monthly buy from one of these restaurant suppliers. They will want you to be on a schedule. They are interested in regular customers. You will need to make it worth their effort. Order as much as your group can afford on a regular basis. If you have someone near town, they will actually deliver!

If your finances are not a problem, there are a few really good sources for pre-packaged supplies. Good name brands are Mountain House, Thrive, Provident, Food Insurance, Wise Company and many more. Thrive has a really cool planner on their website which you can link to from *EffectiveTactics.com*

This planner allows you to set the number of people and the duration you're planning for, how many pre-made meals you want, how much of your plan is to be freeze dried foods, and some other cool options. Thrive isn't cheap. It is very good food though. Even if you can't afford their food (although they offer a monthly payment plan) you can use the planner to see what you need and how much. Buy some things from them and try it out. Mountain House is great too. I haven't tried Provident or Food Insurance myself, but they are well reviewed and recommended by people I trust. You can always buy bulk and package them yourself. This is a bit more work but it is a lot cheaper. Rice, beans, oats, sugar, salt and a lot of the other bulk items can be stored in buckets and jars. You just have to keep the moisture and air out. Cool and dry is your new mantra. There are a ton of great videos and tutorials on how to package your bulk goods. We will cover these in the Effective Tactics podcast. *(See the back cover for details.)*

Make an emergency meal plan. Figure out what things you make now that you can make during a disaster. Start with stocking up on those things. Look at the list. You will also need a grinder mill and some practice cooking with the above ingredients. A good cookbook will do wonders, Such as *Cookin' with Home Storage* by Vicki Tate. There are many out there, but you should own at least one. You need a plan or menu that you can work through. Look at the ingredient quantities used in your menu. Buy accordingly. Adjust your purchasing to fit your diet. Be sure to make the meals as nutritious as possible. Watch your food group distribution. Do not live on beans alone. They may be easy to cook, but you won't be easy to live with. Not to mention the nutritional deficiency you will experience. Here's a silly fact. *YOU NEED FAT*! Yep. You heard me. A diet that is short on fats is unhealthy. Eating unsaturated fats (and small amounts of saturated fats) not only provide your body with energy, but also helps to absorb vitamins. Remember, you're going to have a pretty limited diet. You need to retain all the vitamins you can. Adults should get 25-30% of their calories from fat. Want to know a secret? Peanut butter is great for this. Heck, nuts in general are excellent sources of fat. They store well and fit the bill for fat content. Fat provides nine calories per gram. Carbohydrates only provide four calories per gram. Those in cold weather or performing manual labor will greatly benefit from the substantial energy stored in fats.

There are plenty of places to buy pre-packaged storage foods. Some are less expensive than others. Some are worth the extra money. None of them are as cheap as doing it yourself. Food grade buckets, Mylar bags, desiccant packs, dry ice, Gamma lids... These are all terms that you will become intimate with through this book. Don't be scared by the fancy names or big words, it is pretty easy to do your own bulk storage and one of those infomercial vacuum seal units is really handy for smaller portions.

I'm hungry. Are you hungry? Do you have any idea how much food you eat in a year? You eat a ton of food. No, seriously. The average American eats 2,000 pounds of food every year. Suddenly, I'm not so hungry anymore. We eat an average of 3,800 calories per day. Wow! *Ummm, waitress! Yeah, can I change my order? Yeah, I'll have the salad instead. Thanks.* The average adult needs between 2,000 and 2,400 calories per day. We are eating nearly twice what we need. Now the scary part; that number is down from where it was a few years ago! Do you have a basement? A few REALLY big closets? Where on earth do you plan to store a ton of food? Wait, that's a ton per person in your household. Dwell on that for a second.

Fitness and diet aren't really the focus of this chapter, but I needed to address it briefly. We really need to bring our eating habits under control now, before a crisis happens. The sooner you get your body accustomed to fewer calories, the better off you will be when you're reduced to beans and rice. I say that because beans and rice are some of the easiest and longest lasting food stores you can find.

Here is a primer for food storage. *This is one year of food for one person*. You're going to still be hungry but you won't be starving:

> **Rice - 100 lbs**
> **Wheat - 200 lbs**
> **Oats - 100 lbs**
> **Pinto Beans - 60 lbs**
> **Powdered milk - 25 lbs**
> **Olive oil - 10 quarts**

Honey - 40 lbs
Sugar - 40 lbs
Salt - 30 lbs

You should store a year of multi-vitamins to fill in the dietary gaps.

You should also have roughly 50 pre-prepared meals (MRE, Mountain House, Thrive, etc) on hand. Mostly because the many things that you might be doing all day to survive will take longer, as will cooking. Having ready-to-eat (10 min or less) meals will be a blessing.

Other things to add to break the monotony of the above menu:

Coffee
Teas
Spices
Dried fruits and nuts
Canned foods (meats and veggies)
Hard candies - to help morale.

Canning

This is not my area of expertise. You should really have a garden if possible. If not, plant some fruit trees. Anything to augment your storage will help. Even if you can't have a garden, you should be buying items to can. Fruits and vegetables are crucial, even if you plan on hunting. You need vitamins! This is sad to say, but meat alone is not enough! Did you know that you can can (ha!) meats? Yep! Canned pot roast, roast beef... just about anything can be canned! If you don't get a fancy canning set-up, at least get a good book, take a class, watch some videos, do something to prepare yourself. Buy some canning supplies. Try it. Try jam. It's pretty easy. My wife made plum jam this year. I never had plum jam before now. I was a grape and strawberry guy. *PLUM JAM IS AWESOME!!!* Put it on waffles and then send me a thank you letter. You're welcome. Now, go get some jars and some fruit and get cannin'!

I cannot overstress the need to practice before a disaster. Do you really want to try it in the dark the first time? Do you really want your first meal in the middle of a disaster to be a blind experiment with tools and ingredients you have no practice with? Try a meal a week or a meal a month from your storage foods. It will give you time to add a pinch of this or a dash of that. That way when disaster falls on you and your loved ones, you will have a good foundation of experience to draw from.

Bon Appétit!

Medicine

Over-the-Counter and Prescription Drugs

Getting a cold can be pretty miserable; so can having a headache. Most of us don't suffer nearly as much because there are cold remedies and pain killers in our medicine cabinets. But if you are like me, you allow them to run down or totally out before you buy more. Imagine the unnecessary suffering in the midst of an extended crisis if you haven't stocked extra medications and a cold or flu virus comes along. Just imagine…. Enough said?

Now let's talk about how long drugs can last.... A law was passed in 1979 requiring drug manufacturers to stamp an expiration date on their products. This is the date which the drug is guaranteed to have full potency and safety.

The Food and Drug Administration did a study at the request of the military who had an expensive stockpile of drugs and were facing tossing out and replacing them every few years. The study found that 90% of most drugs, both prescription and over-the-counter, were perfectly good to use even 15 years after the expiration date. Much of the original potency of the drug remained even a decade later.

Essential Oils

In times of crisis, when there is no access to a pharmacy and the modern medicines we have come to rely on, even a simple infection can become deadly. While there are some medicines, like insulin, for which you need to consult with your doctor about storing for emergency, there are alternatives to pharmaceuticals which can address many of the ailments you may need to treat. Essential Oils have been used throughout history for their medicinal and therapeutic properties. Today, people are moving towards more holistic approaches to health and rediscovering the power and effectiveness of high quality Essential Oils. Essential Oils can serve as an antibiotic, anti-bacterial or disinfectant, anti-inflammatory and many other uses which most rely on drug store products to treat. They can be used one oil at a time or in complex blends. Essential Oils are usually administered by one of three methods: diffused aromatically, applied topically, or ingested.

To fully educate and explain to you the many uses of Essential Oils would take a book bigger than this one, and I highly recommend you get a copy of such a book. One I recommend is *A Reference Guide to Essential Oils* by Connie and Alan Higley. It is featured on the **Effective Tactics** website along with a link to the source for Essential Oils I use and endorse. It would be a shame to go to great lengths of preparation for survival only to die from an ordinary infection which could have been treated with an understanding of medicinal resources which have spanned the ages. No serious prepper should go without an understanding and inventory of Essential Oils.

Firearms and Other Weapons

This guide recommends that you own guns. I firmly believe that firearms are an absolute necessity for being prepared. Think of it this way: you don't know how long the situation will last. You may need to hunt for food. People during disasters are willing to do a lot of things, terrible things, for the good of their family. Would you die for your loved ones? Would you kill to protect them, to keep them from starving? You may not, but someone else might. Having supplies *WILL* make you a target in a long term catastrophe. Protect yourself. Protect your family. Protect your supplies.

The things that go bump in the night... Do you fear them? The saying "God made man, but Samuel Colt made them equal" is fairly accurate; but having a gun isn't enough. You need training and practice. If you can't confidently use a gun, you are inviting danger. Remember, safety is the first and most important rule of firearms. Memorize the chapter on firearms function and safety. Make the rules of safety your mantra whenever you are near firearms; teach your children, your family, your friends. Now for the meat of the subject:

Everyone in your group or family that is mature enough, and capable of using safely, should carry a small flashlight and a pocket knife at all times. Everyone in your group should be trained to handle firearms safely. Everyone should be trained to clean and service your firearms. Everyone should be taught the fundamentals of shooting; breathing, sight picture, trigger control, grip, stance and recovery. Everyone should practice enough with each weapon to be comfortable with it and to be reasonably accurate. There should also be some emphasis on shooting under stress. There are tons of great classes out there that can teach these skills. Ask your local law enforcement who they would recommend. I suggest that you consider getting your Concealed Carry Permit as well, but this will be a decision you will have to consider carefully. When deciding on the caliber of your weapons, think about ammo availability. 9mm, .22 cal, .45cal, .223cal/5.56mm and 7.62mm are very popular and ammunition will be easier to find both before and after a disaster.

Weapon Recommendations for Your Family or Group

Small LED Flashlight

(Not exactly a weapon but how do you use a weapon in the dark without one?) Look for something waterproof. You'll probably throw it in the laundry once... My buddy has washed and dried his Thrunite Ti at least three times (that he has told me about). Another great light is the Olight i3s. They use a single AAA battery, offer better-than-average brightness, and have exceptional runtime on LOW setting. The ready availability of AAA batteries makes these a great option. If you prefer a little more brightness and AA battery, look at the Thrunite 1A lights.

Machete

This is a great tool and a viable weapon should it be necessary.

Pocket Knife

A priceless daily tool, many pocket knives carry sentimental value as well. I had my grandfather's old pocket knife with me for many years.

.22cal Pistol

This is great for practice and the ammunition is cheap. Look for a model that shoots the same rounds as your .22 rifle. It will also be good for hunting birds and small game. This might be a revolver or a semi-automatic. If you get a semi-auto, look at picking up several extra magazines for it.

.22 cal Rifle

This will bring home a lot of meals should it come to that. It also gives you a cheap and easy platform to practice shooting skills. Again, look into extra magazines for this as well.

Large Caliber Pistol

Whatever your beliefs, this is a necessity in a survival situation. It will give you protection, food and peace of mind. I'll catch a lot of flak for this, but I think this should be a minimum of 9mm. The truth is this... the gun you have will be infinitely better than the one you don't. Buy several extra magazines and a holster for this one.

Large Caliber Rifle

This should be at least a .223/5.56mm. I would strongly recommend a 7.62mm here. The good news is that you can get a surplus Mosin Nagant for around $150 or so. Should you have a better rifle? Probably. Once again, the gun you have is better than the one you don't. These are known for their reliability and reasonable accuracy.

Shotgun

This should be a 12 gauge, if for no other reason than the availability of shells. This will be an easier way to hunt birds and makes accuracy *LESS* of an issue in a home defense scenario. A mix of buck shot and bird shot is recommended and perhaps a couple boxes of slugs as well. Practice with all three. The recoil difference between them may come as a surprise if you haven't. Run a piece of white medical tape or white paint down the top of the barrel to help aim in low light situations.

Air Rifle

This will be perfect for taking small game quietly. Pellets are cheap and compact. Find a good brand or ask around for the regional favorite. Crossman, Beeman, and Gamo are the local breed where I live.

Bow

A good compound will be hard to beat as the quietest hunter in the forest. Lots of practice is necessary but worth the time invested. A variety of heads will make a bow a very versatile tool.

Blunt Instruments

These include a baseball bat, club, baton or other hand weapon that is used to strike a person.

Pepper Spray

This can be either personal defense, dog spray or bear spray. There are many different types for different applications. Pepper sprays can be serious eye and respiratory irritants. Defensive Devices and Fox are top brands in this area.

You Should Also Have:

- Cleaning and maintenance supplies for each caliber
- Good lubricant and a manual is a must
- Gun safe or trigger locks for every weapon
- Lockable ammunition storage

Check your local laws for restrictions and requirements for all of these items.

These are recommendations. You MUST obey your local laws regardless of the information I provide.

Firearm Safety

Apply the following safety rules in every situation, with any kind of firearm:

1. Always Keep The Muzzle Pointed In A Safe Direction
2. Firearms Should Be Unloaded When Not Actually In Use
3. Don't Rely On Your Gun's "Safety"
4. Be Sure Of Your Target And What's Beyond It
5. Use Correct Ammunition
6. If Your Gun Fails To Fire When The Trigger Is Pulled, Handle With Care!
7. Always Wear Eye And Ear Protection When Shooting
8. Be Sure The Barrel Is Clear Of Obstructions Before Shooting
9. Don't Alter Or Modify Your Gun And Have Guns Serviced Regularly
10. Learn The Mechanical And Handling Characteristics Of The Firearm You Are Using

1.   ALWAYS KEEP YOUR FIREARM POINTED IN A SAFE DIRECTION

Never point a firearm at anyone or anything you do not intend to shoot whether or not it is loaded. This is particularly important when loading, unloading or field stripping the firearm. ALWAYS control the direction of the firearm.

2.   ALWAYS TREAT EVERY FIREARM AS IF IT IS LOADED AND WILL FIRE

Do not take anyone's word that the firearm is unloaded - always check for yourself. Never pass your firearm to another person until the cylinder or action is open and you visually check that it is unloaded. Keep your firearm unloaded and safely stored when not in use.

3.   NEVER RELY ON MECHANICAL FEATURES OF THE FIREARM ALONE

Only your safe firearm-handling habits will ensure the safe use of your firearm. This is your responsibility.

4.   ALWAYS BE SURE OF YOUR TARGET AND WHAT IS BEYOND IT

Always be sure of where the bullet will strike and shoot only where there is a safe back stop free of obstructions, water or other surfaces which can cause ricochets. Be sure your bullet will stop behind your target. Bullets can glance off many surfaces like rocks or the surface of water and travel in unpredictable directions with considerable velocity. Do not fire randomly into the sky.

5.   ALWAYS USE THE CORRECT AMMUNITION FOR YOUR PARTICULAR FIREARM

Never use non-standard, reloaded or "handloaded" ammunition which has not been subjected to internal ballistic pressure testing. There are many reputable reloaders out there; if you know one you can trust or you have the expertise yourself, these may be use with caution. Many things can go wrong in the reloading process. Please be very careful.

6.   IF YOUR GUN FAILS TO FIRE WHEN THE TRIGGER IS PULLED, HANDLE WITH CARE!

This can be caused by one of a couple problems:

A.   *Hard primer* - This is when the primer is struck but fails to ignite. Depending on your firearm, a second pull of the trigger may solve this problem. Then maybe a third. If it still fails to go *"bang!"* as expected, keep the muzzle pointed in a safe direction for at least 30 seconds before removing the round.

B. ***Hangfire*** – This is a delay in the detonation of gunpowder or other ammunition, caused by some defect in the fuse/primer. While "hangfire" is a documented phenomenon (primarily related to contaminants getting into the primer or propellant) it's incredibly rare. You should keep the muzzle pointed in a safe direction for 30 seconds before removing the round.

C. ***Dud*** - is just what it sounds like. The 30 second rule still applies.

Personally, because my primary interest in firearms is defensive rather than sporting, and because people tend to fight like they train, I've decided to take my coaches advice on this, which is to be aware of the possibility, but not to modify the drill because of it. If it doesn't go boom (assuming your handgun has restrike capability), hit it again, right away. If it still doesn't go boom, get one into the pipe that will right away, which means a tap/rack/bang drill. You must decide what is best for you while considering the safety of those around you.

7. ALWAYS WEAR EYE AND EAR PROTECTORS SPECIFIED FOR USE WITH FIREARMS

Wear eye protection that is specified for use with firearms every time you handle your firearm for cleaning and maintenance. Wear eye and ear protection specified for use with firearms every time you discharge your firearm. Make sure others in the vicinity of where you will be shooting do so as well.

8. BEWARE OF BARREL OBSTRUCTIONS

Be sure the barrel is clear of obstructions before shooting. Mud, water, snow or other objects may inadvertently lodge in the barrel bore. A small obstruction can cause a dangerous increase in pressure and may damage your firearm and cause injury to yourself and others.

*****NEVER MANIPULATE, ADJUST OR CHANGE ANY OF THE INTERNAL COMPONENTS OF YOUR FIREARM UNLESS SPECIFICALLY INSTRUCTED TO DO SO IN THE MANUAL THAT ACCOMPANIED YOUR FIREARM***

Improper manipulation of any other internal component may affect the safety and reliability of your firearm and may cause serious injury or death.

*****NEVER ALLOW ANY ALTERATION OR REPLACEMENT OF PARTS IN YOUR FIREARM UNLESS PERFORMED BY A QUALIFIED GUNSMITH USING AUTHORIZED PARTS***

If you do otherwise, improper functioning of your firearm may occur and serious injury or death and damage to property may result. Simple modification like polishing feed ramps, adding accessories or changing external parts should be fine as long as you follow instructions. If you are extremely handy and qualified, changing trigger groups or barrels is not exceptionally difficult. Just use high quality parts and don't be afraid to ask for help from a professional. If

49

you aren't 100% sure of your abilities, find a professional who is willing to teach you how to service and work on your weapon.

9.   MAINTENANCE BEFORE USE

Before using your firearm for the first time, it should be cleaned. See the cleaning instructions that accompanied your particular firearm. Your firearm was treated at the factory with either a preservative or oil to protect it against corrosion during shipping and storage. Preservative and oil should be wiped from the bore, chamber and exposed areas using a clean swab or patch before using the firearm. Purchase cleaning supplies from firearms dealers that are specifically designated for your type and caliber of firearm. Many suppliers offer these in kit form for your convenience. Follow the instructions provided with your cleaning supplies. Whenever your firearm has been exposed to sand, dust, extreme humidity, water or other adverse conditions, it must be cleaned and lubricated.

10. LEARN THE MECHANICAL AND HANDLING CHARACTERISTICS OF THE FIREARM YOU ARE USING

Not all firearms are the same. The method of carrying and handling firearms varies in accordance with the mechanical characteristics of each gun. Since guns can be so different, never handle any firearm without first having thoroughly familiarized yourself with the particular type of firearm you are using; the safe gun handling rules for loading, unloading, carrying and handling that firearm, and the rules of safe gun handling in general.

For example, many handgun manufacturers recommend that their handguns always be carried with the hammer down on an empty chamber. This is particularly true for older single-action revolvers, but applies equally to some double-action revolvers or semiautomatic pistols. You should always read and refer to the instruction manual you received with your gun, or if you have misplaced the manual, simply contact the manufacturer for a free copy.

Having a gun in your possession is a full-time job. You cannot guess; you cannot forget. You must know how to use, handle and store your firearm safely. Do not use any firearm without having a complete understanding of its particular characteristics and safe use. There is no such thing as a foolproof gun.

Kids and Guns

If you have children you must make them "Gun Safe Kids." They should be allowed to touch, use, look at and shoot them. You must supervise them whenever they are with your guns. Satisfy their curiosity. Give them your time, every time they ask. Keeping guns and ammo locked up isn't enough. Curious kids will always find a way. You know your kids. If they are responsible, take them shooting with you. Let them watch for a day. Show them the operation, the safety mechanisms, the liading process... everything. This is your one chance to get it right before you put a gun in their hands. This means that you *NEED* to set a perfect example. They'll be watching closely. I started my kids on BB guns. They needed to exhibit perfect adherence to the rules. No exceptions. If they could show me that they were responsible enough with those, we could move on to some louder tools. Kids need to understand the inherent danger that a firearm presents and have respect for the awesome power that can take a life or save a life. Once they understand, respect and follow the rules, it's time to show them just how much fun can be had. Let them enjoy this great American tradition.

Maintenance before Storage

When storing your firearm, do not encase it in anything that will attract or hold moisture; for example, leather or heavy cloth. Also, do not store firearms with a plug inserted in the barrel because this can be a contributing factor to moisture accumulation. If your firearm is to be stored for an extended period, the bore, chamber and internal surfaces should be oiled with a high-quality lubricating oil or preservative intended for firearms. The external parts, receiver, bolt and barrel, should be coated with an anti-rust oil. Before using your firearm again, be sure to clean it. Every time you clean your firearm, check it for signs of wear. If excessive wear is noted, do not use the firearm. Return it to the manufacturer for service or have it checked by a qualified gunsmith.

Safe Storage and Transportation

YOU ARE RESPONSIBLE FOR YOUR FIREARM AT ALL TIMES

In owning a firearm, you must undertake full-time responsibility for your firearm's safety and security. You must protect yourself and all others against injury or death from misuse of your firearm 24 hours a day. You must secure firearms safely from children and unauthorized users. Your firearm should always be kept unloaded and locked when not in use. A weapon in "stand by" for use in self defense is not included here.

A lock, when properly used, can be an effective tool in preventing unauthorized access to your firearm. However, never assume that the use of the lock alone is sufficient to safely secure your firearm. There are other alternative locks and safe storage containers available in the marketplace which may also be appropriate for your particular needs. Consult your local gun shop, hardware store or local law enforcement agency for guidance on the variety of other safe storage devices or practices which may be appropriate for your particular needs. You must always evaluate your personal situation and employ the security systems that meet your needs to prevent children and unauthorized users from gaining access to your firearm.

NEVER LOCK A LOADED FIREARM AND NEVER LOAD A LOCKED FIREARM! NEVER LEAVE THE KEY TO THE LOCK FOR YOUR FIREARM WITH THE STORED FIREARM! ALWAYS STORE YOUR FIREARM AND AMMUNITION SEPARATELY.

Firearms and ammunition should be stored separately so that they are not accessible to children or other unauthorized persons. Safe and secure storage of your firearm and ammunition are your responsibility. It is a full-time responsibility. You just need some way to keep children, who haven't been taught how to properly use firearms, from loading it. Examples are a locked ammo can, a separate safe or a locking cabinet.

NEVER ASSUME THAT A "HIDING" PLACE IS A SECURE STORAGE METHOD.

Others may be aware of your storage location or come upon it by chance. It is your personal responsibility to use common sense when storing your firearm and ammunition and to always make sure they are not accessible to children or other unauthorized persons.

Firearms are not cheap. They do not respond well to pure neglect. They are tools designed to put food on the table, provide security in times of danger and to possibly save your life. They deserve to be respected as such. Take care of your guns so that when the time comes, they can take care if you.

I have included a shooters log in the Appendix to track your practice and range time. Copy and put it in your range bag or safe and take it with you when you shoot.

Barter Supplies and Skills

This is a list of items and abilities that will be very valuable in a prolonged crisis. These are *EXTRA* items you should set aside for trade should you find the need to barter. Bartering skills for goods will be a huge benefit to you and your group. Find a new hobby that you can use to benefit your future.

- Water and bottles
- Water purification
- Food
- Alcohol
- Salt
- Coffee and tea
- Medical supplies
- Fire starting supplies
- Medical training
- Gardening skills
- Security training and experience
- Toilet paper
- Feminine hygiene products
- Welding
- Heirloom seeds
- Gunsmithing
- Firearms and ammo
- Ammo reloading skills and supplies
- Sewing/seamstress
- Sources of energy, batteries, solar, wind/water generator
- Electrical/solar installation and repair
- Butchering
- Vitamins
- Carpentry/construction
- Fuel and fuel preservative
- Tools
- Gloves
- Livestock
- Fencing supplies and tools
- Engine repair
- Latrine supplies (lye)
- Cigarettes

- Building materials
- Socks
- Ham radio and operations
- Canning supplies
- Bee keeping
- Rope
- Canning skills
- Sugar and honey
- Baby supplies
- Children's clothing
- Gold< Silver, Pre 1965 coinage
- Storage bags / ZipLock
- Aluminum foil
- Candles and candle making supplies
- Soap, bleach, cleaning supplies
- Personal hygiene supplies

Investing in Precious Metals

There are a vast number of scenarios in which paper currency can lose value or become worthless and where the most common form of purchasing (plastic cards) would be completely useless. Investing and storing Precious Metals is another important step in being fully prepared for any emergency, crisis or economic fallout. There is peace of mind that comes from owning Silver and Gold, which you can physically hold in your hand and that is universally recognized as valuable. Precious Metals have survived inflation, deflation, financial crises and natural calamities over the centuries. They are portable, fitting easily in your pockets or bug out bags, and they won't degrade.

Gold and Silver have both been used as money. Gold has traditionally been the standard while Silver is relatively inexpensive, often referred to as "Poor Man's Gold." This simply means its currency that can be easily owned and used for most basic transactions. Silver was actually the original monetary standard in the United States, with a U.S. dollar being defined as 371.25 grains of pure Silver or 416 grains of Standard Silver.

In the event credit cards and paper money lose their value, you will be glad to have invested in Precious Metals as it may be the only form of currency you can count on. Another method of storing Silver is pre-1965 Silver coinage. These coins contain 90% Silver. These coins are generally referred to as "Junk Silver." Buying Gold Bullion can be cost prohibitive for some. Junk 90% Silver provides an affordable alternative. The smaller denominations make for easier bartering than larger Silver Bullion or Gold Bullion coins or bars. Keep an eye on your pocket change and look through that old Mason jar in the corner. According to current prices, the value of just four pre-1965 quarters is at about $14.00; not bad for a buck's worth of pocket change. Many precious metals brokers/businesses offer Junk Silver for purchase. The amount you should purchase depends on what you can afford, as with any of the items I suggest you store, but a good rule is to buy as much as you can. Food, shelter and sustainability are the priority, but if it REALLY hits the fan and you need something, barter or Silver/Gold will be your only options. With that said, there is a theoretical point in a crisis where Gold may not even buy food. Life truly is more precious.

There are three recommended ways to store your precious metals and I suggest a combination of all three for maximum safety: Purchase a safe-deposit box from a bank and store some of your Precious Metals in it. You may want to hold the box under the name of a limited liability company that you have formed, this will help you keep your name off your valuables. Next, store a portion of your Precious Metals in a fireproof safe in your home, hidden in a place you can easily access and inside a storage container that can be quickly tossed into your Bug Out Bag. Bury the last portion of your metals in a waterproof container outside. Dig a hole on your own property at least three feet deep. Never bury your Precious Metal on government property or any property besides your own. You won't have any rights to it in the event someone finds it.

Provident Precious Metals (www.ProvidentMetals.com) is the company I recommend for purchasing your investment metals because they are honest and have great prices; and because they support our veterans through the minting and sales of the Love Your Veterans coins featured in the ad at the front of this book (which I always carry to remember and show appreciation to our heroes!) Provident Metals also has a great section for food storage and other preparedness products on their website.

EFFECTIVE TACTICS

supports
LoveYourVeterans

*If you aren't willing, to do as much for freedom at home as our soldiers do abroad, you have failed as a citizen. I carry a lot of things in my pocket every day, and when I get up in the morning, my **Love Your Veterans** coin goes in first thing, before my wallet, before my pocket knife, before my flashlight, that coin goes in first! –Todd Jones*

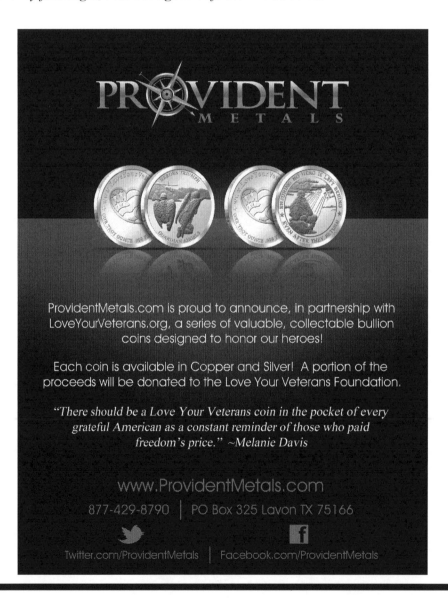

POWER-BATTERIES-LIGHTING

Power

How long does a disaster last? An hour? A week? A month? How long did people go without power during Katrina? How long after Sandy? How long could you go without power to your home? How long will the food last in your refrigerator? Do you know how to open your garage door when the power is out? (Hint: It's the little handle that dangles down. You know...the one you hit your head on every time you're carrying something fragile.)

Nearly two million people lost power in the Gulf States as a result of Katrina, with power companies estimating that it would take more than several weeks to restore power to some locations. After 23 days, only 75% of customers had power restored. In south eastern Florida, 1.3 million customers were also without power for weeks. New York and New Jersey fared better after Sandy. It still took 13 days to get 95% of power restored.

As for the goodies in the fridge... four hours is the time the majority will last with a power outage. Most meat and dairy are at or near their safe temperature limit. Some items will keep for a lot longer and some of the things in your fridge never needed to be kept cold. The best trick is to keep the door closed.

Do you have a generator? Always thought they were too expensive, didn't you? How much is all the food in your fridge worth? A basic generator that is just big enough to run the fridge and charge your cell phone, battery charger (also for your flashlight and radio batteries) and a radio can be bought for a couple hundred dollars. It can power more than that, just not simultaneously. A 2000 watt generator is about right for the average refrigerator and a few accessory devices. We even run a large space heater off of one. If your budget allows, look at the Honda EU series or the similar ones from Yamaha. They are very quiet and ultra efficient. Their fancy inverter system provides power that is clean enough for more delicate electronics like laptops etc. Most regular generators provide very "dirty" power, meaning that the output fluctuates greatly and more sensitive electronic devices are not fond of them.

Keep fuel and a spare spark plug handy. Stabilize the fuel with Stabil or PRI-G to allow for longer storage life. Buy a couple of extension cords and a power strip to go with your generator. Also look into small to medium solar kits for your battery charging needs. If you can afford a full solar system for your house, you will be miles ahead of the game.

Batteries

RECHARGABLES ARE WORTH EVERY PENNY!!! There, I said it. Hope you recover from the shock. Now listen up, Sparky, everything you thought you knew about rechargeable batteries is old news (most likely). The new Li-ion (Lithium ion), Li-Po (Lithium Polymer), and Ni-MH

(Nickel Metal Hydride) batteries available today are really amazing. They offer faster charging times, better storage life and more charge cycles, (i.e. how many times you can recharge the battery) than ever before. The Sanyo Eneloop batteries are wonderful. Look at some of the chargers from Nitecore, XTAR, and SysMax. They charge a wide variety of batteries and do everything *automagically*! They can also charge different types and sizes simultaneously. Now brace yourself, I'm about to geek out for a second. This is where cool batteries and awesome flashlights meet. If you want maximum brightness and runtime from your new flashlights, look for ones that will run on both traditional batteries (AA, AAA, CR123) and the new higher voltage Li-ion rechargeable ones. Normal alkaline batteries are usually 1.5 volt, some rechargeable batteries are 1.5 volt or 1.2 volt. Here is the cool part: a 14500 Li-ion is usually 3.7 volt and the same size as a AA. A 10440 Li-ion is also 3.7 volt but it is AAA sized. Look for flashlights that will use either and you have a win/win situation. You can pick up some Li-ions for daily use. You will have a much brighter light and usually longer run time and still have the ability to use off the shelf alkaline batteries in a pinch. My one bit of advice from the "done it the wrong way" files... look for Li-ion batteries marketed as "Protected." That means they have a little circuit that shuts them off if you drain them down too low. This can damage the battery and destroy its longevity. Buy "Protected" batteries and quit worrying.

Lights

I feel the need to come clean about a personal problem I have... I am a *Flashaholic*. There, I said it. I feel better now that everyone knows.

FLASHAHOLIC: noun -

Someone who appreciates and actively seeks information about portable lights because of an ongoing fascination with them and their development; and whose interest often results in the purchase and/or modification of these lights, very often to the point of distraction, social alienation, drunkenness, impoverishment and general disintegration.

Yep, that's me.

Close your eyes... Can't see much, can you? Would you want to walk around like that? Would you want to defend yourself like that? Cooking dinner, walking the dog, fixing the car, checking the breaker box, building a fire and many other tasks become exponentially more difficult in the dark. If your power goes out in a storm, where are your flashlights? I get up in the morning and put one in my pocket and it doesn't leave my side until I crawl back into bed. It's small, light, rechargeable and extremely bright for a light that uses a single AAA battery. Do you still own a MagLight, MiniMag or other "ancient" technology flashlight? Even the new MagLED lights are terribly underpowered. Don't get me wrong, they are incredibly well made. They are just a slow moving company when it comes to lightning technology. The new elements are smaller, lighter, brighter and much more efficient. I own a pocket-sized flashlight that is not only 3-4 times brighter than my 3-D cell MagLight, but it will run for 240 hours on one AA battery. I won't tell you which lights to buy. I'll tell you some great manufacturers to try, but you need to decide what lights fit your needs. I will tell you that you need a variety. They will serve different purposes. Look for lights with different output levels. This allows you to fit the brightness to the task. I will also tell you that if you aren't using rechargeable batteries, you are throwing money away.

Necessary Lights

EDC or Every Day Carry- is a pocket-sized light that you carry every single day. Do you know when the power might go out? Do you know when an earthquake or other disaster might strike? Having a light within reach to find your way to safety or to signal rescuers may just save your life or someone else's. Look at lights that use a 1-AA or AAA battery. It's also a good idea to keep at least one spare battery handy. You will be surprised at how often you will use this light.

Car Light- This can be a little larger. It will allow for longer throw (beam distance) and longer runtime. Because it can be put in a glove box or console and forgotten for years, I recommend using lithium batteries and keep them *with* the light and not *in* the light. Most electronics have a small but continuous drain on batteries and lithium batteries have a 10 year or longer shelf life. I would look for a light that uses 2-AA batteries.

The Nightstand Light- This is the big daddy. A thrower king, the sun in your hand, the blinder of all that is evil! Yep, a defensive light. This one isn't going to be cheap. That being said, there are plenty of options that are more affordable. Here you are looking for a light with a larger head diameter and a high "lumen" output. There is a geek-out moment here too, but I'll save you from it. 500 lumens should be a minimum. Many lights in the $30-50 range offer upwards of 800 lumens. Solarforce L2 lights are a great affordable start. For less than $50 shipped, you can get the light, charger and two batteries from eBay. I own three of these. They are also a 1" diameter body and offer a pressure switch for weapon mounting. The best options in this category will use both

CR123 batteries or an 18650 Li-ion. The CR123 batteries are expensive and not rechargeable but they are available in a lot of stores. They are a lithium battery so they will have that great 10 year shelf life.

The Headlamp- Not just for coal miners and dentists anymore, these are vital to give you hands-free illumination; unless you prefer the taste of a good flashlight... The problem is that after a while of holding a light between your teeth, your jaw gets tired and you might drool on your project. Here are some different options to consider:

- Batteries in a belt pack to make the unit lighter on your head
- Red or green LED bulbs to limit visibility
- Various output modes for brightness or to flash S.O.S.
- Velcro or elastic straps for comfort
- Look for one that uses the same type of batteries as another light in your collection
- Floodlight or spotlight? Some spotlight models offer a diffuser (frosted plastic cover) to act as a floodlight

If a complete headlamp is not in your budget, there are some great headbands for smaller lights. My wife and kids all use the NiteIze headband. It is a simple velcro headband with an elastic loop to hold your EDC light. I use the Klarus version. Nitecore also makes a nice one with a top strap. The Nitecore is under 15 dollars and the Niteize and Klarus are under eight bucks. It's a great alternative to spending $40 or more on a good headlamp. It might encourage you to spend a bit more on your EDC light.

Some great lights are available from *Olight, Thrunite, Trustfire, Solarforce, Streamlight, Surefire, 5.11, 4Sevens, Jetbeam,* and *Nitecore.* There are some other great brands out there but I have had good luck with all of these.

Now go buy a bunch of lights!

I'll see you at the next *Flashaholics Anonymous* meeting!

GLOSSARY

Here you will find descriptions of some of the items found on the kit lists. These are not alphabetical. They are grouped in this order:

First Aid, Fire, Utility, Food, Signaling, Navigation, Communications, Lighting, Power and Repairs

First Aid

FAK – First Aid Kit. S. FAK=Small First Aid Kit, M =Medium, L =Large or home-sized kit.

Quick Clot or Celox – These are granules that cause rapid coagulation to stop bleeding fast. They come in various sizes, even a small household size for those kitchen or tool mishaps.

Feminine Hygiene Products – Having these for their intended purpose is good enough, but think about what they are for… a tampon makes a heck of a plug for a bullet wound and a "pad" makes for a super absorbent bandage for larger cuts. Either way, you'll look like a hero for having them.

Benadryl – *Only use this method when medical treatment is NOT AVAILABLE AT ALL*. I am not a doctor. This was the recommendation from a friend in emergency medicine. This is for the treatment of anaphylactic shock. Bee Stings, insect bites or food allergies (nuts, shellfish, etc...) fall into this category.

Diphenhydramine (Benadryl) Syrup - Take two capfuls of diphenhydramine syrup and gargle for one minute, then swallow. The goal of this improvised treatment is to keep the throat from swelling shut due to the anaphylactic reaction and to get the antihistamine into the bloodstream. If you do not have the syrup, but have tablets or capsules, you can still make use of the drug. Chew the tablets and then put some water into your mouth and gargle the drug and water solution. If you have capsules, open and mix them with water or any available liquid and gargle the solution.

Iosat Potassium Iodide - Blocks the thyroid's absorption of cancer-causing radioactive iodine released from a nuclear reactor or nuclear bomb. If this is on your list of concerns...get some. It's not perfect, but it is effective and affordable.

Dental Kit – This should contain items for general dental hygiene as well as storing a product like DenTemp. DenTemp is an emergency tooth filling agent; it can be used to fix a lost filling, broken tooth or loose or missing crown. A dental pain reliever is also a good idea.

Fire

Tinder-Quik – Nearly waterproof tinder that is simple to "fluff" and lights easily.

Fresnel Magnifier – This can be used to start a fire (with some patience and a clear day) or to aid in reading small print on your gears instructions.

Wind and Waterproof Matches – Larger than regular stick-type matches, these give off a ton of flame to light your well prepared tinder. It is designed to stay lit in damp or moderately windy conditions.

WetFire Tinder – Really cool tinder that you crumble up and spread on your fire base to catch sparks, it lights very easily and will even burn on water!

Flint and Steel – These are very durable fire starters. A steel striker usually has a protective paint on its surface; scrape this off before you begin. Use long, firm strokes with the "toothed" side of the striker, for best results.

Steel Wool – 0000 (four aught) Steel wool is really handy for a lot more than cleaning. It can be used as a debris filter for dirty water. It will polish most types of soft to medium metals and works wonders on stainless steel and chrome. Its importance here is as a fire starter. Loosen it up a bit and place some small tinder on top. Then hold a 9 Volt battery or the leads from a pair of jumper cables (other end connected to the car) and voila!!! Try it some time. It's a pretty cool reaction to watch.

Fire Extinguisher – Type ABC extinguishers are the best for general purposes. This will cover most of the fires possible in your home or car. These will put out fires of combustible materials (wood, paper, cardboard), fuel, oil, grease and electrical fires. As you can imagine, most fires are of more than one type at once. An ABC extinguisher has you covered. Water has a horribly good chance at making the fire worse unless you have a lot of it. Unless you're a firefighter with a truck and a hose, stick with the extinguisher for the job.

Utility

Duct Tape – Yes, average, ordinary, everyday duct tape. Better still is the newer Gorilla Tape. This also comes in a compact 1" width. It is super handy for a wide variety of tasks and repairs. Priceless if you need it.

Full-Sized Pocket Knife – This should be a folding pocket knife with a blade of between 3 and 4 inches (check your local laws). This should be easy to open with one hand and have a stout pocket clip. Look at a lot of these. Play with them; see how easily they open. Check out the blade quality and the type of steel. This should be a pretty good quality blade. Expect to spend at least $30 here. Many knives run well up into the hundreds of dollars. I don't see the need to spend that kind of money, although it may have its merits. Columbia River, S.O.G., Boker, Kershaw, Smith & Wesson and Gerber are all great brands that make knives in every price range. There are tons of companies I have missed here. Research it a bit and choose wisely. This may be your new best friend. Are you looking for a knife in the upper price range but not willing to "Pay for the name?" Look into Emerson knives (Emersonknives.com). These are the best "Hard Use" knives around. Worth every penny!

Leatherman Squirt – I won't tell you what full size multi-tool to buy. Just buy a good quality one and spend at least $30 on it. A small multi-tool, on the other hand...BUY THIS ONE! I have owned a lot of other brands in this category. Leatherman Squirt wins; ease of use, build quality, tools included, small size, spring loaded pliers. (Scissors and wire strippers are also available.) This is the way to go. I use it more often than my full size tool and I carry both all day, every day.

Gerber Artifact – This is an awesome little tool; part prybar, part knife, part screwdriver, part bottle opener. I use this thing so often, I can't believe I didn't buy one sooner. I used it earlier today... twice. It comes with extra #11 blades too. Kill two birds with one stone.

Scalpel Blades – Or the hobby blades that come with the Gerber Artifact. #11 straight edge or #22 curved blades are both recommended. These are easier to adapt to tasks in the field than razor or utility blades.

Insert Snare Kit – This will be for trapping small animals. It has rings on the ends of steel cable to create a locking loop. It can also be used as the steel utility wire for tie-downs, binding handles, or other projects in place of paracord or string; put one end into a stick for a handle and tie off with string.

Steel Utility Wire – Pre-made snare kits work as well or better. They can be used where paracord is not strong enough.

Paracord – Also known as 550 cord or seven strand cord, it has seven smaller "strings" inside an outer sheath. Known for its strength, paracord has a billion uses. The inner strings can be used for fishing or sewing repairs. Buy high quality cord. Cutting corners here will just frustrate you later.

Kevlar String – This was cheaper than I thought it would be. eBay has it for less than $20 for 1000ft of 100 pound test line. It comes in ranges from 50-200 pound test. 100-150 pound should serve most of your purposes here.

Aloksak Waterproof Bag – These are much more than a sandwich baggie. Durable and genuinely waterproof, these come in several sizes from one that fits a cell phone or radio to one that will hold a rifle or two. They make a nice 12'x12' size that will work well for protecting your important documents pack. Since they are waterproof, you can use them to store filtered water if need be.

Dry Sacks – These come in various sizes and can be found at sporting goods stores or online. These will help keep your gear clean and dry in all sorts of conditions. When empty, they roll up pretty small. They can also be used to keep wet or dirty items away from the rest of your gear. Remember to turn them inside out and let them dry after holding wet items. You can also use them to hang a bag of food (Bear Bag) out of reach of critters. Hang this far enough away from your camp that you are also not a part of the menu.

Food

• •

Fishing Kit – These can be found pre-assembled from places like *AplusSurvival.com*. Otherwise you should include: 4 weights/sinkers, 2 swivels, and a 4 hooks in a small kit with 20-50' of 10 pound test line. Time to look for worms and grubs!

One Liter Water Bottle – This should be the hard plastic (Nalgene) type. It should have a wide mouth opening. This can be used for water when needed but also works well as watertight/airtight storage. I keep three in my *Go Bag*. Most of my small items and fire starting gear are stored in them.

Open Fire Cooking Grill – Just like it sounds; a round or rectangular grill to be placed on bricks or stones, over a fire, for cooking. You can steal the one from your BBQ if you need to but an additional one would be handy if you still have propane for the BBQ. Look for one that is pretty heavy duty. It will need less support and last longer than the cheapo version.

Aluminum Foil – Buy quality, heavy duty aluminum foil. It can be used for cooking, a heat shield, reflector, to carry water or to boil water. The possibilities are awesome. Be sure to pack at least three sq. ft. of it. Fold it carefully.

Signaling

Signal Mirror – This will be used for long distance signaling (up to 20 miles). Look for one with an aiming port in the middle.

Whistle – It should be fairly compact and light; and needs to be loud enough to get the attention of rescuers nearby. A multipurpose unit that holds matches, tinder and has a compass can be a space saver. You can also wrap your duct tape around the body to further save space.

Orange Flagging – The little rolls of orange ribbon can be used to make signals for aircraft (an arrow to indicate your direction of travel), as a trail marker to find your way back to a camp or location, or to mark your location to be seen from the air or the ground.

Navigation

20mm Survival Compass – Don't buy the cheapest one you can find. This will be affordable enough as it is. It won't be fast and it will react poorly near metal, but it will be useful in the absence of a full-size unit.

Map Measure and Pedometer – These are priceless items when navigating by map on foot. The map measure will allow you to calculate the distance to your destination and a pedometer will help to approximate the distance traveled.

Full-Sized Sighting Compass – The Brunton 8099 is a phenomenal example of this... pricey but perfect. There are a lot of similar compasses out there to be found, but the Brunton is the benchmark. The Brunton F-8040G is another great compass for half the price. There are many quality compass manufacturers out there. I only have experience with the Bruntons.

Pocket GPS – This should always be used with a map of the area (if available). Compare and plot your course on the real map as well. Do not rely solely on the electronics for when the batteries die or you trip and smash your little toy... you'll be lost. Another thing to consider is that in a massive disaster, GPS may not be reliable. Here is a little snippet I found on a forum and it makes sense:

"WHY NOT GPS? I had the same thought when reading these lists- aside from the fact that it runs on batteries, it is a greatly dependent system. The satellite constellation and the ground based WAAS stations are dependent upon a working infrastructure and stability. Who has trouble surviving when everything is working right? If the SHTF scenario is ugly enough, that GPS unit is a liability if anything. It can be used to track you. It can go offline in a second, or it can be used

to give erroneous information. It's actually in the Federal Aviation Regulations that the US gov reserves the right to distort the data as it sees fit 'in the interest of national security' and we all know what a rabbit hole that is."

Lighting

Streamlight NANO – Ultra small LED flashlights are bright for their size. They have a clip to attach them to gear and bags. It takes the tiny LR41 watch-type batteries so carrying extras is easy. The NANO can be found for less than $10.

Long Run LED Flashlight – Look for a light that uses batteries common to your other devices. This will make extra batteries easier to carry and share. That being said, look for a light that has a "LOW" setting with a runtime greater than 30 hours. The Thrunite line is awesome for this; bright enough on "HIGH" for most tasks but with "LOW" setting runtimes well over 100 hours on a single AAA or AA battery. The Thrunite Ti XP-E is the AAA version for around $25 or so and the Thrunite 10T is the AA version for around $35. It is well-made, waterproof, and compact. There are a ton of great lights out there. Look around *Candlepowerforums.com*. Just watch out. You might become a "Flashaholic." You might want to look at a larger, brighter flashlight as well. The new technology in flashlights is amazing; more light, better distance, and better battery life than ever before. I gave all of my Maglights away.

12 Hour Chem Lights – Glow sticks, as they may be better known, are as useful for light as they are for signaling or trail marking. Tie a string or paracord to one end and swing it in a circle over your head or in front of you, to signal aircraft or search crews, in low light.

Communications

Two-way Radios – These should have a range of at least 25 miles. This is a best case scenario. Most times these will reach 10-15 miles. You should find units that take standard (AA or AAA) rechargeable batteries. Proprietary batteries will be harder to charge, replace, or substitute than standard batteries. Get at least three radios for your kit. Scouting/hunting parties should have a minimum of two radios and home base should be able to communicate with them as well.

Hand Crank Radio – AM/FM/Weather band radio for news and entertainment. Look for one that has solar as well. Some even have a USB output to charge cell phones or GPS units. Eton and C. Crane both make great units.

Ham Radio – Amateur Radio, often called "ham radio," has consistently been the most reliable means of communications in emergencies when other systems fail due to power outages and destruction of communication facilities. By selecting the proper frequencies, hams can talk across town, throughout the state or around the world. They demonstrate the truth in the saying, "When all else fails, ham radio works!" You must have a license to operate a ham radio and most communities set up training and licensing as part of their emergency preparedness plan.

Power

Batteries – NEVER!!! NEVER store a device with alkaline batteries installed. Almost all devices have parasitic drain; meaning that they consume a little power even when turned off. If you are lucky, you will only have dead batteries when you try to use your device. If you aren't lucky... the batteries will have leaked all over the inside of your device and possibly ruined it. Whenever possible, use rechargeable or lithium type batteries in your flashlights and other devices. Alkalines are fine in an emergency; just don't count on old ones being good.

Battery Charger – This should charge many types of battery (AA, AAA, C, D, etc.) and charge several at a time. Power may be scarce or time sensitive. You need to get the most "bang for your buck" when using a generator to power one of these. This might not always be the case, but it is better safe than sorry.

Solar Battery Charger – With the same story as the regular charger, store lots of types and several at a time of solar batter chargers. It will take a long time to charge items by solar power but it's better than running around in the dark with a dead flashlight.

Generator – This should be at least a 2000 watt unit. This will power a few household items. The refrigerator will need most of this on start-up, but use less than ½ of that to run. You could plug in the TV and satellite receiver or other small items as needed. You cannot run a whole house on this size. Contact a licensed electrician to see what size generator you would need for that level of usage. If you want to run all or part of your home with a generator, there are some great solutions from Generac or Reliance Controls. These are usually called a transfer switch or transfer panel. This will disconnect you from the "Grid" safely and allow you to power all or some of the circuits in your home off your generator. This will ensure that there are no big surprises when the power in your neighborhood comes back on! You should still have a more portable generator for smaller uses and to take with you should you need to evacuate. In the smaller generator arena, the Honda EU series is small, ultra-efficient and very quiet. This is what we use. It starts easy and runs great. Be sure to use preservative on the fuel for these. The carburetor jets on these are tiny and gum up easily with old, untreated fuel. Trust me on this one...cleaning the carb, on the kitchen table, by flashlight, during a snow storm can really cause some frustration and a few curse words…. at yourself for knowing better. Yamaha makes a similar line of generators to the Honda EU series.

PRI-G and PRI-D – This is the best fuel treatment system you can get your hands on with relative ease. From what I understand, this is what the military uses. It gives you up to a 10 yr storage life on fuel and can even be used to bring old fuel "back to life." Look for Power Research Inc. at Priproducts.com

Power Inverter – These clever little devices turn your car into the generator. These come in many sizes. Smaller ones can be run off a 12 volt cigarette lighter port. The larger ones need to be hardwired to the battery with larger wiring. They come with instructions on what size wire you will need. Remember that this is not free power. You will have to run your car to power these. While smaller and usually cheaper than a generator, these are probably not a viable replacement for one. That being said, if you have a whole house generator, this might be a good back up.

Repairs

Sewing Kit – Again *AplusSurvival.com* comes through with a great compact kit. I have one for travel as well. Other versions of these can be found at most department stores. Heck, our Dollar Store has one. Needles, thread, buttons, safety pins, and a needle threader are included in most.

Tarps/Plastic Sheeting – This is for repairs to your roof, windows, doors, etc... This can also be used to "shelter in place" or seal off a room in case of chemical attacks or accidents. It won't be perfect, but it's better than not having a plan.

Tyvek or Painters Suit – For working with hazardous material to protect skin and clothing, look for a waterproof suit. Test that whatever you are using does not react with your suit before proceeding. A pair of rubber boots would go well with this.

Roof Patching Compound – A tar-like substance for fixing roof leaks and can be used to fix small cracks in many surfaces to create a wind proof /waterproof seal. This comes in one and five gallon paint cans.

Misc. Lumber and Plywood – You should have a dozen 2x4 and 2x6 pieces of lumber on hand. Eight foot pieces should cover you for most repairs. I also recommend a couple of pieces of ½" or ¾" plywood. This can be used to fix the roof, walls or doors if you get minor storm or earthquake damage.

RESOURCES AND CREDITS

I need to recognize some of the sources of information, descriptions and equipment. In my experience with them, they have been top notch companies and have great gear. Some of the books on the list, I've yet to read, but people I've talked with during this adventure have highly recommended that I get these as well as recommend them to you. So, here it goes:

Websites

EffectiveTactics.com- Where you can listen to our internet radio show recordings, organized in specific categories. The show covers prepping and self defense topics and is always current.

Facebook.com/pages/Effective-Tactics/500051513376469 – Our Facebook page.

Twitter.com/EffectiveTactic – Our Twitter page.

Blogtalkradio.com/effectivetactics – Our Blogtalk page. Find all of our podcasts here as well, though not organized by category.

WeaponsTrainingSchool.com - Great place for CCW classes, shooting instruction and tactical training in Northern California; Great People, Great Classes, Great time!

Youtube.com/user/NutNFancy – Great resource for gun and gear reviews from a veteran. This guy has his head on straight, is easy to understand and does a great job of sharing good, unbiased information.

ShieldTactical.com – Phenomenal company. They do so much for veterans and helping out during disasters. Look them up. They carry a ton of great gear.

ThriveLife.com – Complete food storage solutions and a great planner system.

ThriveLife.com/planner/thrive/setup/ - Here is the planner. Even if you don't get the food from them, their planner will help you with the basics. Their food is really good. You should try it.

OPSGEAR.COM – Awesome gear. Awesome Deals. Awesome company. Awesome support. And they're pretty nice people too.

BlackTydeTactical.com – Excellent BOB bags at great prices. Also their tactical and security gear is top notch.

CandlePowerForums.com – Great source to research the latest technology in flashlights. If your light is more than three years old, you owe it to yourself to look at the new toys coming out. Beware... you might become a flashaholic like me.

LDS.about.com/library/BL/faq/BLCalculator.htm – Yep, the address is a pain but the resource is great. Want to know how much food you need to store for your family? This is it.

Thrivelife.com/food-rotation-systems – Great food storage rotation systems which keep your can storage fresh.

LockNLoadJava.com – Drink coffee? Support our troops? Good, go here and place an order for you and them!

AplusSurvival.com – Great eBay store as well as their website. They carry most of what you'll need. Prices are great as well as fair shipping. Tons of FAK supplies.

MultiTaskerTools.com – The absolute best multi-tool out there. Pricey but worth every penny

Ciscostrading.com – These guys carry some nice essential gear and tools at great prices. **They support out troops, so please support them!**

SurvivalMetrics.com – eBay store and website. These guys have great complete kits. They also leave a bit of room for you to add the things they didn't. Their kits are sold by a lot of other websites and in some stores as well. I used their descriptions for some of the items in the GLOSSARY.

Bedgunsafe.com – Great hidden gun safes and storage.

Libertysafe.com – I have a friend who is a professional locksmith and safe technician...this is not only what he recommends, but also what he owns. P.S. He says don't buy an electronic keypad model...too many problems. (Small safes with a keyed bypass are ok.)

Pendletonsafes.com – These are really well made and amazing designs, bright enough to see inside!   Awesome!

MaydayIndustries.com – Lots of pre-made kits and some supplies as well as great tips in their small guide book.

Sawyer.com – Best water filtration ever. The Point ONE filter can make up to <u>540gal/day@ 0.1 micron</u>. This is the filter that is saving lives, in third world countries, every day. Online store is - <u>www.sawyersafetravel2.com</u>

1800Prepare.com – Go-Bags, Office Kits, First Aid Kits. They make a nice "Bucket Latrine Kit".

Camelbak.com – Great water carrying solutions and phenomenal backpacks

GunRightsAcrossAmerica.com – Do you want to protect your Second Amendment rights? Go here and get involved!

GunOwners.org – Another excellent organization protecting your Second Amendment rights. "The only no-compromise gun lobby in Wasington" –Ron Paul (R-Tex)

BePrepared.com – Some Nice Kits, Great source for food, CANNED BACON!!!

Budsgunshop.com – Firearms, cleaning supplies, and accessories at great prices

CampingSurvival.com – Good resources and a decent book selection

Coghlans.com – Outdoor, camping, and survival gear

EmergencyLifeline.com – Full kits, food bars, water pouches, and Search & Rescue Kits

MountainHouse.com – Freeze dried foods, meals and supplies. Prepackaged -just heat and eat for most items.

ProvidentLivingCenter.com – FOOD- Lots of food, cookbooks, and kitchen supplies

LAPoliceGear.com – Great source for backpacks, blades, boots, and great clothing. Prices are incredible. Great closeouts section.

AdventureMedicalKits.com – Best First Aid Kits (FAK) around.

EmergencyPreparednessSupplies.net – Good variety of items.

Google Search – Secure Logic Wall Vault – Awesome design for behind artwork or in a closet. Pretty cool design and affordable. Key bypass too

Slickguns.com – Great deals on firearms

ActionTarget.com – Great reusable steel targets. Good prices and really well buil.

DefensiveDevices.com – pepper spray and other protection goodies

Gerberblades.com – Great multitools, knives, and the Bear Grylls survival kits

www.TinHatRanch.com - great site for preparedness info from a guy with the right plan, mindset and skills. He also has a great YouTube channel under Tin Hat Ranch.

Try to spend your money locally. If you can't find it in or around your area after a REALLY good search, Wal-Mart, eBay, Amazon, and these websites above are all good sources. Just remember... cheap gear may not be the quality you hoped for when you need it the most.

Books

• •

Disaster Prep 101 – Paul Purcell, 2004, InfoQuest

Petersen's Field Guides to Edible Plants (regional) – Lee Allen Petersen, 1999, Houghton Mifflin Harcourt

Crisis Preparedness Handbook – Jack A. Spigarelli, 2002, Cross-Current

SAS Survival Guide – John Wiseman, 2009, William Morrow

Emergency Food Storage & Survival Handbook – Peggy Layton, 2002, Clarkson Potter

The Survival Handbook – Colin Towell, 2012, DK Adult

The Survival Medicine Handbook – Joseph Alton M.D., 2013, Doom and Bloom LLC

Emergency Food in a Nutshell – Probert/Harkens, 2006, Emergency Essentials

Preparedness Now! - Aton Edwards, 2009, Process

Disaster Preparedness and Awareness – Mayday Industries.com

The All New Cookin' with Home Storage – Peggy Layton, 2000, Gold Leaf Press

Homesteadingsurvivalism.myshopify.com – This is a webpage but they offer some great books on CD-ROM. Great prices too.

Patriots – James Wesley Rawles, 2012, Ulysses Press

When Disaster Strikes: A Comprehensive Guide for Emergency Planning and Crisis Survival - Matthew Stein, 2011, Chelsea Green Pub.

One Second After – William R. Forstchen, 2011, Tor Books

Reference Guide for Essential Oils – Connie and Alan Higley, 2013, Abundant Health Publisher

KIT APPENDIX

EDC – Every Day Carry

CAR KIT

CAR TOOLS

GO-BAG/BOB Bug Out Bag

IMPORTANT DOCUMENTS

HOME KIT

HOUSEHOLD ITEMS

FOOD

FIREARMS AND OTHER WEAPONS

SHOOTERS LOG

FAK - FIRST AID KITS

      S. FAK Small Kit

      M. FAK Medium Kit

      L. FAK Large Kit

EDC KIT

What You Have Is All You Get

Sometimes, you end up alone and all you have is what's in your pockets. When you end up in such a situation, the equipment or items that you left in the vehicle or back at home are useless to you. They might as well not even exist other than to motivate you to get to them. There are items that you will need should disaster strike. The simple solution to making sure that you have all the items you need is to make a habit of carrying these items every day and everywhere you go. We refer to these items as an everyday carry or EDC kit. Our plan is to use an EDC kit to either get you home (to either stay or get your BOB) or to get you to your car (and it's CAR KIT). By having a layered approach you cover more contingencies without lugging your BOB on your back 24/7. I actually carry a small EDC bag with some regular everyday items. Inside is my EDC kit. Should I need to ditch my bag, my EDC kit is easy to grab and stuff in a pocket or clip to a belt loop. (yes, that was a tip...put a carabiner on it)

Here's a quick list of some suggested items.

ITEM	REC. QTY	ON HAND	SHELF	PURC ON	EXP DATE	SOURCE/COST
Waterproof Pouch						
Leatherman Squirt multi tool						
AAA LED flashlight						
Space Blanket or similar						
Pocket Knife						
Whistle/Matches/ Compass/ Combo						
Paracord 550lb test						
Small Roll Duct Tape						
Gerber Shard or Artifact						
P-51 Can Opener						

ITEM	REC. QTY	ON HAND	SHELF	PURC ON	EXP DATE	SOURCE/COST
Scalpel Blades						
SuperGlue						
Small First Aid Kit						
Ziplock Sandwich Bag						
Water Purification Tablets						
Mini Sharpie or Pencil and Paper						
Small Carabiners						
Latex/Nitrile Gloves						
Cable Saw/Snare kit						
Cash and Coins						

ITEM	REC. QTY	ON HAND	SHELF	PURC ON	EXP DATE	SOURCE/COST
Non Lube Condom (to store water)						
1/3 Hacksaw Blade						
Signal Mirror						
Small Zip Ties						

NOTES

CAR KIT

This kit should be in your car at all times. There should be one in each car if possible. It is intended to get you home or to a safe place.

ITEM	REC. QTY	ON HAND	SHELF	PURC ON	EXP DATE	SOURCE/COST
Approx. 2700-3000cu.in. Backpack	1					
Full Sized Multi-Tool	Over $30					
1Ltr. Water Bottle	2					
Several Fire Starting Methods	3					
Water Filtration Kit	1					
Full Sized Sighting Compass	1					
Regional Map	1					
Tube Tent or Tarp W/ Tent Stakes	1 + 4					
Paracord	50'					
M. FAK	See List					
Long Run LED Flashlight + Batts	1 + 2 sets					
Duct Tape	50'					

ITEM	REC. QTY	ON HAND	SHELF	PURC ON	EXP DATE	SOURCE/COST
Signal Mirror	1					
Gerber Shard/Artifact	1					
Kevlar String	100'					
Bivvy Bag	1					
Butane Lighter	1					
Crank Type Radio	1					
Extra Socks	1pr					
Energy Bars (5yr shelf life)	2-2400 calorie					
1" Gorilla Tape	1 roll					
Scalpel Blades	3					
Snare Kit	3					
Fishing Kit	1					
Sewing Kit	1					
Mini Sharpie and paper	1					

ITEM	REC. QTY	ON HAND	SHELF	PURC ON	EXP DATE	SOURCE/COST
Pocket GPS and Batts	1 + 2 sets					
Aluminum Foil	3 sq ft					
P51 Can Opener	1					
Superglue	1					
Ziplock Bags	4					
HD Trash Bags	2					
Latex/Nitrile Gloves	2pr					
Folding Saw wood/ plastic/metal	1+1 blade ea					
Small Carabiners	4					
Handcuff Key	1					
Collapsible Water Container	1 gal plus					
Zip Ties	various sizes					
10x Monocular	1					
Leather/Work Gloves	1pr					

ITEM	REC. QTY	ON HAND	SHELF	PURC ON	EXP DATE	SOURCE/COST
Magnifying Glass	1					
Poncho	2					
12hr Chem Lights	4					
Knife Sharpener	1					
Siphon Hose	4'					
Emergency Blanket	1					
Orange Flagging	100'					
Survival Guide	1					
Road Flares	2					

NOTES

CAR TOOLS

X	ITEM
	Fire Extinguisher
	Fix A Flat and 12 Volt Tire Compressor
	Jumper Cables
	Snow Chains
	Tire Repair Kit
	Short Tow Strap
	Radiator Hose Repair Kit
	Set of sockets and wrenches
	Screwdriver Set
	Folding Shovel
	Duct Tape
	Pliers
	Vise Grips
	Spare Fan Belt
	Work Light (LED, 12 volt, Rechargeable)
	Work Gloves and Rubber Gloves
	Road Flares (4) and 12hr Glow sticks (4)
	Heavy Duty Garbage Bags (2) to be used as a tarp or poncho
	Glass/Window Breaker
	LocTite
	Bailing Wire (20ft)
	Wire Cutters/Strippers/Crimpers with assorted connectors
	Electrical Tape and 12 ga Electrical Wire (10')

NOTES

GO BAG
or
B.O.B.

This kit should be with you anytime you take a long trip. If you can't make the roundtrip on one tank of fuel...TAKE IT WITH YOU! If you have to evacuate... TAKE IT WITH YOU! This kit is designed to get you and one other person safely to your destination.

ITEM	REC. QTY	ON HAND	SHELF	PURC ON	EXP DATE	SOURCE/COST
Approx. 2700-3000cu. in. Backpack	1					
Full Sized Multi-Tool	1					
1Ltr. Water Bottle	2					
Several Fire Starting Methods	3 minimum					
Water Filtration Kit	1					
Full Sized Sighting Compass	1					
Regional Map	1					
Tube Tent or Tarp W/ Tent Stakes	1 + 4					
Paracord	50'					
M. FAK	See List					
Long Run LED Flashlight + Batts	1 + 2 sets					
Duct Tape	1 roll					
Signal Mirror	1					
Gerber Shard/Artifact	1					

ITEM	REC. QTY	ON HAND	SHELF	PURC ON	EXP DATE	SOURCE/COST
Kevlar String	100'					
Bivvy Bag	2					
Butane Lighter	1					
Crank Type Radio	1					
Extra Socks	2 pr					
Energy Bars (5yr shelf life)	6					
1" Gorilla Tape	1 roll					
Scalpel Blades	3 minimum					
Snare Kit	3 minimum					
Fishing Kit	1 kit					
Sewing Kit	1 kit					
Mini Sharpie and paper	1					
Pocket GPS and Batts	1 + 2 sets					
Aluminum Foil	3 sq. ft.					
P51 Can Opener	1					
Superglue	2 tubes					

ITEM	REC. QTY	ON HAND	SHELF	PURC ON	EXP DATE	SOURCE/COST
Ziplock Bags	4 of 2 sizes					
HD Trash Bags	2					
Latex/Nitrile Gloves	2 pr					
Folding Saw wood/ plastic/metal	1 + 1 ea blade					
Small Carabiners	4					
Handcuff Key	1					
Collapsible Water Container	1 – 1 gal					
Zip Ties	10					
10x Monocular	1					
Leather/Work Gloves	1pr					
Magnifying Glass	1					
Poncho	1					
12hr Chem Lights	3 minimum					
Knife Sharpener	1					
Siphon Hose	4' minimum					

ITEM	REC. QTY	ON HAND	SHELF	PURC ON	EXP DATE	SOURCE/COST
Emergency Blanket	1					
Orange Flagging	1 roll					
Survival Guide	1 small size					
Emergency Candles	3 minimum					
Full Sized Pocket Knife	1					
Large Fixed Blade or Machete	1					
Hard Candies	a few					
Headlamp LED + Batts	1 + 1 set					
Travel Size Toilet Paper	1 roll					
Feminine Products (if applicable)	3 minimum					
Climbing Type Rope	100'					
Small Knot Tying Guide	1					
Wide Brim Hat	1					
Dry Sacks	3 minimum					
Mosquito Headnet	2					

ITEM	REC. QTY	ON HAND	SHELF	PURC ON	EXP DATE	SOURCE/COST
Rat Trap	2					
2 Way Radios	3 minimum					
Tablet Washcloth	2					
Folding Shovel	1					
Small Prybar	1					
Small Hammer	1					
Hand Warmers	2					
1 Change Clothing	2 sets/1 ea					
Sunglasses	2 pr					
Extra Prescription Glasses	1ea if necessary					
Camp Cup (stainless steel)	1					
Hikers Stove and Fuel	1 + 2 sets					
Insect Repellant	1 sm can					
N95 Face Mask	2					
Bailing Wire	20'					

ITEM	REC. QTY	ON HAND	SHELF	PURC ON	EXP DATE	SOURCE/COST
Plastic Grocery Type Bags	2					
Hacksaw Blade	1					
Lt Weight Rain Gear (not cheapo)	1ea					
Family Info and Contact Kit	1 set					

NOTES

IMPORTANT DOCUMENTS

These are the documents that you will need copies or duplicates of.

These should be in an Aloksak or waterproof pouch. This should be in your go-bag and a second set somewhere out of your home.

Keep this with friend, family member, safe deposit box, or at a vacation home.

Keep this package in a locked box or other secure storage. These will be of infinite importance should they be needed after the situation has subsided.

Check off items here as they are added to the kit.

X	ITEM
	Contact info for your family/group
	Emergency out of area contact info
	Cellphone numbers, Radio frequencies, Contact time schedule for your group
	Birth Certificates
	Passports
	Drivers License
	Marriage Certificates
	ID Cards
	Military Service Records
	Child/School ID
	Adoption, Foster Care Papers
	Immigration Papers
	Legal Will, Living Will, Power of Attorney
	Inheritance Documents
	Deferred Payment Records
	Immunization Records
	Medical Prescriptions
	Medical Insurance Paperwork
	MediCare/MedicAid Paperwork
	Loan Papers (Home/Auto/RV/Bank, etc...)
	Titles/Deeds
	Mortgage
	Vehicle Registration/Title
	Lease/Rental Agreements
	Home/Auto/Business Insurance
	Home Inventory (Photo/Video, with serial numbers if possible)
	Property Taxes
	Banking Info (Checking/Savings/CD)
	Safe Deposit Box Info
	Credit Card Statements

X	ITEM
	Pay Stubs
	Investment Portfolio/Retirement/Pension
	Social Security Documents
	Tax Returns
	Business Records
	Business License
	Business Lease/Property Records
	Business Equipment/Inventory Records
	Employee Records
	Diplomas
	Training and Certification Records
	School Records
	Firearm Licenses
	Firearm Make/Model/Serial Numbers
	Family Photos and Videos (saved on disc or USB device)

NOTES

HOME KIT

These are the items you should have packed in bins at home. These are EMERGENCY ITEMS.

Try not to use them. If you do have to break into the kit, replace the items on your next trip out. Don't wait! You'll forget. I know you...you'll forget. So just stay out of it.

This is a list of the items that you should keep stored in a cool dry place in your home. These are household items, tools, supplies, food, firearms, and repair necessities. You should take as much of this kit with you as possible should you need to relocate or evacuate.

ITEM	REC. QTY	ON HAND	SHELF	PURC ON	EXP DATE	SOURCE/COST
Water Collection and Storage Kit	Water page					
Lanterns and Fuel	2 + fuel					
Camp Stove, Fuel, and Cooking Kit	1 + fuel					
Flashlights and Batteries	2 min					
Battery Charger (Solar and Electric)	1 ea					
Firearms Kit	See List					
Generator and fuel	1 min					
Fuel + PRI-g or PRI-d treatment	25gal min					
Fire Extinguisher ABC Type	3					
Oil (auto, 2 cycle, and tool oils)	1 qt each					
Extension cords med and heavy duty	300 ft total					

ITEM	REC. QTY	ON HAND	SHELF	PURC ON	EXP DATE	SOURCE/COST
Fuel Siphon or 4 ft Hose	1					
Open Fire Cooking Grill	1					
Latrine Kit	1 per 4 people					
Shovels	2					
Duct Tape	3 rolls					
Axe/Maul/Wedges for Firewood	1 ea					
Knife and Axe Sharpening Kit	1 ea					
Tarps Various Sizes	4					
Plastic Sheeting 10x25 and 20x50	2 ea					
Hammer (Claw and Small Sledge)	1 ea					
Nails and Screws Various Sizes	Bunches					

ITEM	REC. QTY	ON HAND	SHELF	PURC ON	EXP DATE	SOURCE/COST
Staple Gun and Staples	1 + 3 boxes					
Camp Shower Kit	1					
Work and Rubber Gloves	2 pr ea					
Hand Saw	1					
Hack Saw	1					
Glues, Caulking, Adhesives	3 ea					
Rope	100 feet					
Bungee Cords various sizes	12					
Bailing Wire	1 roll					
Kevlar String (remainder of roll)	1000 ft					
3M N95 Filter Mask	1 per person					
Tyvek or Painters Suit (waterproof)	1 per person					

ITEM	REC. QTY	ON HAND	SHELF	PURC ON	EXP DATE	SOURCE/COST
Screwdriver Set	1					
Pliers/Vise Grips/ Plumbers Wrench	1 ea					
Channel Lock Pliers	1 large 1 small					
Gas Wrench	1					
Bung Wrench	1					
Measuring Tape	1					
Misc Lumber for Repairs	See Glossary					
Hand Drill	1					
Prybar	1					
Chain or Cable Lock (for generator)	1ea					
0000 Steel Wool	1 pkg					
Cordless Drill	1					
Chain Saw	1					

ITEM	REC. QTY	ON HAND	SHELF	PURC ON	EXP DATE	SOURCE/COST
12 Volt Power Inverter (1000w min)	1					
Electrical Wiring, Connectors, Tape	25' + Misc Kit					
Roof Patching Compound	1 Can					
Nylon and Vinyl Patch Kit	1 ea					
Tents to match the size of group	varies					
Sleeping Bags	1 per person					
Regional Maps for Location A and B	2 ea					
Binoculars 12x50 Min	1					
Map Measure and Pedometer	2 ea					
Handheld Radios	1/person					
Ham type radio	1					

NOTES

HOUSEHOLD
ITEMS

X	ITEM
	Large Storage Bins (3 – 4)
	TOILET PAPER !!!!! TONS OF IT!
	Latrine Kit
	Feminine Hygiene Products
	Clothes Line and Pins
	Wash Cloths, Towels, Blankets, Sheets
	Books, Guides, Maps, Bible, Coloring Books, Paper
	Pens, Crayons, Markers, Pencils, and Sharpener
	Word Games, Board Games, Playing Cards, Small Kids Toys (if applicable)
	All Purpose Cleaner
	Plain Bleach (unscented, uncolored)
	Laundry Soap
	Shampoo and Bar Soap
	Deodorant/Anti-Antiperspirant
	Toothbrushes and Tooth Paste, Dental Floss
	Moisturizing Lotion and Sunscreen
	Lip Balm
	Insect Repellant
	Anti-Bacterial Foot Spray
	Extra Shoe Laces
	Listerine Mouthwash (Alcohol type) for disinfectant and for oral infection
	Dental Emergency Kit for pain relief and emergency fillings
	Shaving Kit (his and Hers)
	Cotton Balls
	Coffee Filters, Coffee, Creamer, and Sugar Packets (sealed packages)
	Spare Lithium Batteries (Much longer shelf life than alkaline batteries)
	Dish Rags, Sponges, and Steel Wool
	Hard Candies and Treats
	Pre-Packaged Drink Mixes
	Lockable Box for Valuables and Important Documents
	Emergency Medical Guides
	Survival Guides, Regional Gardening Books, Home Repair Guides

NOTES

FOOD

This is one year of basic food for one adult. You will survive, but you will still be hungry.

ITEM	REC. QTY	ON HAND	SHELF	PURC ON	EXP DATE	SOURCE	COST
Rice	100 lbs		30				
Wheat	200 lbs		30				
Oats	100 lbs		30				
Pinto Beans	50 lbs		30				
Powdered Milk	25 lbs		20				
Olive Oil	10 Qts		10				
Honey	40 lbs		indefinitely				
Sugar	20 lbs		30				
Salt	20 lbs		indefinitely				
Grinder-mill							
Multi Vitamins	1 yr supply						
Pre Prepared Meals	50		25				
Coffee							
Various Spices							
Supplement with dried fruits and canned foods as needed.							

NOTES

FIREARMS AND OTHER WEAPONS

These are recommendations. You MUST obey your local laws regardless of the information I provide.

I have included a shooters log to track your practice and range time. Copy it and put it in your range bag or safe and take it with you when you shoot.

The things that go bump in the night... Do you fear them? The saying "God made man but Samuel Colt made them equal" is fairly accurate but having a gun isn't enough. You need training and practice. If you can't confidently use a gun you are inviting danger. Remember, safety is the first and most important rule of firearms. Memorize the chapter on firearms function and safety. Make the rules of safety your mantra whenever you are near firearms. Teach your children, your family, your friends. Now for the meat of the subject.

Everyone in your group or family's that is mature enough, and capable of using safely, should carry a small flashlight and a pocket knife at all times. Everyone in your group should be trained to handle firearms safely. Everyone should be trained to clean and service your firearms. Everyone should be taught the fundamentals of shooting. Breathing, sight picture, trigger control, grip, stance, and recovery. Everyone should practice enough with each weapon to be comfortable with it and to be reasonably accurate. There should also be some emphasis on shooting under stress. There are tons of great classes out there that can teach these skills. Ask your local law enforcement who they would recommend. I suggest that you consider getting your Concealed Carry Permit as well, but this will be a decision you will have to consider carefully. When deciding on the caliber of your weapons, think about ammo availability. 9mm, .22 cal, .45cal, .223cal/5.56mm, and 7.62mm are very popular and ammunition will be easier to find both before and after a disaster.

Recommendations for your Family or group:

Small LED Flashlight - (not exactly a weapon but how do you use a weapon in the dark without one?) Look for something waterproof. You'll probably throw it in the laundry once... My buddy has washed and dried his Thrunite Ti at least three times (that he has told me about). Another great light is the Olight i3s . They use a single AAA battery, offer better than average brightness, and have exceptional runtime on LOW setting.

Machete – great tool and a viable weapon should it be necessary

Pocket Knife – Priceless daily tool. Many carry sentimental value as well. I had my grandfathers old pocket knife with me for many years.

.22cal Pistol – this is great for practice and ammunition is cheap. Look for a model that shoots the same rounds as your .22 rifle. This will also be great for hunting birds and small game. This might be a revolver or a semi-automatic. If you get a semi-auto look at picking up several extra magazines for it.

.22 cal Rifle – This will bring home a lot of meals should it come to that. It also gives you a cheaper and easy platform to practice shooting skills. Again look into extra magazines for this as well.

Large caliber pistol – Whatever your beliefs, this is a necessity in a survival situation. It will give you protection, food, and peace of mind. I'll catch a lot of flack for this, but I think that this should be a minimum of 9mm. The truth is this...The gun you have will be infinitely better than the one you don't. Buy several extra magazines and a holster for this one.

Large caliber rifle – This should be at least a .223/5.56mm. I would really recommend a 7.62mm here. The good news is that you can get a surplus Mosin Nagant for around $150 or so. Should you have a better rifle? Probably. Once again, the gun you have is better than the one you don't. These are known for their reliability and reasonable accuracy.

Shotgun – This should be a 12 gauge. If for no other reason than the availability of shells. This will be an easier way to hunt birds and makes accuracy LESS of an issue in a home defense scenario. A mix of buck shot and bird shot is recommended. Perhaps a couple boxes of slugs as well. Practice with all three. The recoil difference between them may come as a surprise if you haven't.

Run a piece of white medical tape or white paint down the top of the barrel to help aim in low light situations.

Cleaning and maintenance supplies for each caliber.

Good lubricant and a manual is a must.

Gun safe or trigger locks for every weapon.

Lockable ammunition storage.

Check your local laws for restrictions and requirements for all of these items.

ITEM	REC. QTY	ON HAND	Make/Mod	SERIAL #	Purch on	SOURCE	COST
.22 cal Pistol							
.22 cal Rifle							
Lg Cal Pistol							
Lg Cal Rifle							
Shotgun							
.22 cal Ammunition	2000 rds						
Pistol Ammunition	1000 rds						
Rifle Ammunition	1000 rds						
Shotgun Shells	200 rds						
Pistol tools and cleaning kit							
Rifle tools and cleaning kit							
Shotgun tools and cleaning kit							
Extra Magazines .22 cal	4						
Extra magazines Pistol	4						
Extra Magazines Rifle	4						
Speed Loader for Revolver	if needed						
Magazine Loader	ea Caliber						

NOTES

SHOOTER'S LOG

Copy this log and take it with you when you go to the range
or any other shooting activity

Date	Location	Firearm	Caliber	Round Ct.	Notes

NOTES

Love Your Veterans
SHOOT-A-TH⊕N

2014

AIM TO SUPPORT OUR VETERANS

THEY SHOT FOR YOU
NOW SHOOT FOR THEM

Develop your skills and support our veterans at the same time! Go to *Love Your Veterans.org* to find your closest **Shoot-A-thon** or learn how you can be a liaison to help your local range host an event.

FAK

These will be your three sizes of first aid kits (FAK).
Small (S.FAK), Medium (M.FAK), Large (L.FAK)
These will obviously get bigger as you go up in size,
but the L.FAK will be your everyday kit for around
the house. Just don't forget to restock it!

S. FAK

Small First Aid Kit

ITEM	REC. QTY	ON HAND	SHELF	PURC ON	EXP DATE	SOURCE	COST
Bandages various sizes	8						
Triple Antibiotic Ointment	2						
Alcohol Prep Pad	2						
Butterfly Bandages	4						
Medical Tape	1 sm roll						
Pain Relievers 2 types	4 ea.						
Superglue	1 tube						
2x2 pads	2						
Moleskin	sm kit						
Knuckle Bandage	2						
Electrolyte Tabs or Emergen-C	2						
Combat Gauze	1						
Tourniquet	1						

NOTES

M. FAK

Medium First Aid Kit

ITEM	REC. QTY	ON HAND	SHELF	PURC ON	EXP DATE	SOURCE	COST
Bandages various sizes	12						
Triple Antibiotic Ointment	6						
Alcohol Prep Pad	6						
Butterfly Bandages	12						
Medical Tape 2 types	1ea						
Pain Relievers 3 types	8 ea						
Superglue	2						
Combat Gauze	3						
Tourniquets	3						
Larger Bandages	4						
Smelling Salts/ Ammonia	2						
Small ACE Bandage	1						
Gauze	sm roll						
Thermometer	2						
Tweezers	1 pr						
Safety Pins	4						
Mole Skin	1 set						
Latex Gloves	2pr						
Anti-Itch Cream	1						
Sunscreen	2						
Anti-Diarrheal	4						
Suture Kit	1						
2x2 pads	4						
Knuckle Bandage	4						

NOTES

L. FAK

Large First Aid Kit

ITEM	REC. QTY	ON HAND	SHELF	PURC ON	EXP DATE	SOURCE	COST
Bandages	36						
Triple Antibiotic Ointment	8						
Alcohol Prep Pad	8						
Butterfly Bandages	24						
Medical Tape 3 types	2ea						
Pain Relievers 3 types	36 ea						
Superglue	4 tubes						
Larger Bandages	12						
Combat Gauze	6						
Tourniquets	6						
Smelling Salts/ Ammonia	4						
ACE Bandages 2 sizes	2ea						
Gauze 2 sizes	2ea						
Thermometer Digital and Glass	1 ea						
Tweezers	1 pr						
Safety Pins	4						
Mole Skin	2 sets						
Latex Gloves	4 pr						
Anti-Itch Cream	4						
Sunscreen	8						
Anti-Diarrheal	24						
Suture Kit 2 sizes	2 sets						
Compression Dressing	2						
Quick-Clot or Celox	2 sizes						

ITEM	REC. QTY	ON HAND	SHELF	PURC ON	EXP DATE	SOURCE	COST
Rubbing Alcohol	sm bottle						
Betadine	4						
Scissors/Shears	1 pr						
Scalpel kit handle and blades	1 hdl / 4bld						
Forceps	2 types						
Hemostats	1						
tongue depressors	4						
Wound Probe	2						
Prep Pads	12						
Eye Pads	2						
Eye Wash	1 bottle						
2x2 pads	8						
Burn Cream/Gel	8						
Knuckle Bandages	8						
Splint Material	various						
Trauma Pads	4						
Stethoscope	1 book						
Feminine Pads and Tampons	lots						
Cold Medicines (pill form)	24						
Decongestant	24						
Benadryl	24						
Antibiotics if avail	lots						
Dental Kit	2 sets						
Iosat Potassium Iodine Kit	2 kits						
Emergency Surgical Guide	1 book						
Medicinal Plant Guide regional	1 book						

ITEM	REC. QTY	ON HAND	SHELF	PURC ON	EXP DATE	SOURCE	COST
Emergency first aid guide	1 book						
Electrolyte tabs or Emergen-C	10						
Oral I.V. Kit	8						
disposable razors	2						

NOTES

INDEX

Made in the USA
San Bernardino, CA
15 February 2015